SUMMER
SKOOL

SUMMER SKOOL

Teachers – It's an Education.

<small>PUPILS - 40 WAYS THEY'RE GOOD AT BEING BAD.</small>

Edmund Irons

Matador
9 Priory Business Park,
Wistow Road, Kibworth Beauchamp,
Leicestershire. LE8 0RX
Tel: 0116 279 2299
Email: books@troubador.co.uk
Web: www.troubador.co.uk/matador
Twitter: @matadorbooks

ISBN 978 1785892 363

British Library Cataloguing in Publication Data.
A catalogue record for this book is available from the British Library.

Printed and bound in the UK by TJ International, Padstow, Cornwall
Typeset in 11pt Adobe Garamond Pro by Troubador Publishing Ltd, Leicester, UK

Matador is an imprint of Troubador Publishing Ltd

DEDICATED
TEACHERS...

Teachers, if anyone ever...ever... suggests that you have taken the easy career option, then please direct them to the *Summer Skool.*

Contents

Summer Skool – a whimsical look at classroom behaviour, the stresses and the strains many teachers have to face, in spite of (perhaps because of) well-meaning behaviour management policies, school systems and the support of school leaders.

And as our story comes to an end…

OK, men, steady advance now. Shoulder to shoulder.

What the… ? I'm not going in there, Sir.

Can't turn back now, men. One final push to our final objective. That's all. Soon be over. Everything terminates here.

No, Sir, don't want.

Don't wimp out, boy. Last week's intake took it like men. Listen now to the VP.

OK, gentlemen. Line up there ready to enter. Can you bring him to the front?

Sobbing, Moaning.
Silence. Odd Intake of Breath.

Stand tough, men! You'll warm to this, trust me. Crack troops at the ready. Any volunteers? Need four to start; who's SAS material? Best feet forward.

Hesitant Shuffling.

Steady, men. Deep breath, you four. Ready yourselves. Go.
GO! GO! GO!

Let's do it. Just go in!

Door Opening. Clanking Gets Louder.
Occasional Whoosh and a Blast or Two.

Thud as Door Closes.

OK, now the rest of you wait a moment 'til they're dealt with.
STOP RIGHT THERE!! **YOU! Come back!!**

Not goin' in, Sir. Leggit, lads.

Get him, Godfrey.
Dragging Sound, Shoes Across Concrete.

Foreword

Teachers. Why ARE so many pupils good at being bad?

It's tough going for teachers. 40% of newly-trained British teachers are reported to quit within five years; 40,000 left the profession last year. Do school leaders, parents, and politicians really understand the stresses and impossible workloads our education system places on the newly-trained, classroom teacher?

In some Union surveys, 70% of committed teachers cite low-level disruption as a major frustration that often makes them think twice about their chosen career. Curiously, low-level misbehaviour seems rife no matter where in the country a school is located. From Bangor to Bridlington, from Caithness to Kent, pupils seem to employ very similar distraction tactics. Indeed, most pupils have them off to a tee. Some child psychologists and educationalists may well maintain that such skills come naturally? But as any teacher might argue, skilful learning can only result from skilful teaching. And this raises a further question of how, when and where do pupils learn these finer arts? Perhaps, they attend secret classes.

Underlying *Summer Skool's* humorous, fictional approach are serious, factual issues: Mr Godfrey's onerous school day is based on actual timesheets (politicians please take note); and all of the highly creative pupil tactics at Summer Skool – pupil ploys teachers might look out for, particularly during their early careers – can be observed in classrooms daily.

Despite the tribulations, teaching can be one of the most stimulating, rewarding of professions. *Summer Skool* hopes to reassure those new to education to stick with it as initially all teachers undergo the same annoying diversions; also our story might amuse our more experienced colleagues who seemingly effortlessly take it all in their stride.

Engagement

At first, when I confiscated the device, I had no real idea what I was about to unearth. Nor, as a teacher, how devastating it would prove to be.

I'd often pondered why most boys did not seem too keen to learn the things that I, and the school and the education authorities, wanted to teach them. Important things. From the curriculum. Topics they might find interesting... as I do. Useful subjects that they would need in later life. For jobs. Maybe to go to university.

Jack's brightly coloured MP3-type player (which probably had some new-fangled name I hadn't yet come across) just had to be confiscated. School Rule Number 15Cii. Moreover, if any doubtful files should be suspected, like photos or recordings of classmates and teachers, then the device should be handed immediately to an assistant head or a line manager to check its content. School policy suggests that the school's Leadership Team would fully support classroom teachers with any reasonable confiscations; they'd sanction the offender and delete any felonious files.

Of course, we ordinary mortal teachers are reluctant to confiscate anything, it just adds to the workload and it's something else for us to lose. Explaining why you've lost it could involve heads, parents, governors... the list goes on and on. Heaven forbid, the teacher might end up paying for a new one, probably the next generation device with even more features to distract.

Better to quietly tell the pupil to "put it away otherwise it will go". But I didn't. I duly followed school procedures, confiscated said device, and handed it to Humphreys, who swiftly handed it back mumbling Ofsted and "do it yourself and inform his parents if necessary".

With a straight run of eight consecutive lessons to teach, a Parents Evening, and two sets of Year 8 reports before my next free period (Thursday), I somehow forgot about Jack's MP3-thingummy. This is most unusual for a teacher, not because most teachers aren't forgetful, but because most pupils won't let you forget. At Break. During Lunch. After-school. "When can I have it back?" Often the reminder comes at you from different directions. Via an advocate "When can Jack have his… (MP3-thingummy) back?" followed by the implied threat that if he doesn't get it back soon, then somehow Jack might become a burden to the school not only during, but long after classes have ended for the day.

"He needs it to get home."
"What, an MP3 player?"
"It's not an MP3 player, Sir, it's the latest XYZ – it's really important. His mother will go mad."

So teachers don't forget such things. But Jack, a normally well-behaved Year 7, new to the school, didn't protest any further. Perhaps he was too embarrassed. Perhaps he was scared. Anyway, it was after-school the following Friday as I checked my desk to discard the week's uneaten sandwiches that the device resurfaced.

Now it's a common misconception outside the teaching profession that teachers on a Friday night

Go to wild parties,
Go to the gym,
Catch up on marking.

Friday evenings are for collapsing. Collapsing. Swilling wine. Watching TV with one eye closed. Any vintage, any programme. Either eye. And so it was lunchtime on the Saturday when my curiosity again turned to the MP3-thingummy. I clicked one or two buttons, tapped the screen a bit, and eventually came across a menu of the things Jack had been recording. It read:

The Roman Invasion of Britain
Reach Level 5 Maths in a Week
Animals of the Rainforest
Summer Skool 2014
The Best 50 Wordsearches
(what else?)
Great Scientific Discoveries
The Best of One Direction

Apart from the last one, I was impressed. Jack was the conscientious type I'd come to recognise. Why had I confiscated the poor boy's MP3? Nothing on the list seemed to have been recorded during my lessons. Slight apprehension. Guilt feelings. I'd hand it back to Jack on Monday.

By the side of each title there was a security symbol, a lock, and an indication of whether the file was audio, video or something called WMV or Xvid. Jack had left most of the files unlocked.

Curiosity got the better of me. I tried my own subject. Good stuff. Impressed. Relevant. The speaker on the recording really knew my subject. No doubt Jack had scoured the Net for such gems. Well done, Jack. Initiative in bounds. Then, merely out of curiosity in case it contained more of my subject I tapped *Summer Skool – Audio*.

And my life changed.

It was the start of something that would influence my lesson planning, classroom management, and my very future as a teacher. Forever. *Summer Skool* would put schoolboy behaviour into perspective, including things that had previously seemed so illogical. Inadvertently I may have uncovered the meaning of life, classroom life, no less.

Where do boys learn their seemingly natural waywardness? Shoddy parenting. Surely not? No, in hindsight, it's now pretty obvious that most boys, sometime between Years 6 and 7, ages 10 to 12, must get the special kind of training Jack received – secretly, surreptitiously, unknown to their teachers, the education authorities, their parents.

I've transcribed Jack's tape almost word-for-word. I'm assuming he recorded the lectures without the Skool's organisers knowing; under the desk so to speak. It covers five days of lectures which, going by the pupils' reactions in the recordings, seemed to have enthralled, enthused and engaged them in ways most teachers would love to emulate. And learn the boys did; so well that I see signs of the Skool's teaching every day in my classroom. Probably you'll see them in yours also.

I hope that my transcription will help parents and teachers to understand better their sons and pupils, respectively. At the very least it might improve our understanding of what really is happening in our 21st Century classrooms. Finally, due to music licensing agreements and that kind of thing, I've only been able to mention the titles of the stirring tunes the boys marched out to. Insightful lyrics, every one; well worth Googling or YouTubing any legal downloads.

I've gone on far too long. So welcome to the world of hovering Heads and hoovering NEWTs, RETs and RITs, Awesomes and SAGs. Never heard of them? I bet they're around somewhere in your school. Ready? Or as the ADVP might say "Good to go? " Let's get started. It's time to enter the secretive, possibly enlightening, world of the *Summer Skool*.

Edmund Irons

Transcription of Jack's Summer Skool Audio File.

Day One

The boys learn their 3Ss. Why secondary school learning might just be secondary. Enter the silent assassin.

Welcome.

Welcome Gentlemen. Oh, I see some of you seem surprised. Bit disorientated perhaps, are we? No you are not in the wrong place. This is The Summer Skool for Boys. And I am pleased to see so many of you here, nice and early; indeed most of the eligible boys from town. Just finished Year 6 and raring to embark on a fresh adventure at your new secondary school. No doubt, all looking forward to the many exciting challenges.

Confused by the title *Gentlemen*. Please don't be. I use this title only because it's likely to be the one most often used by teachers to address you during your secondary education.

Yet, GENTLEMANLY conduct is the least we want to see from you. Quite the opposite. From now on your mission is to cause as much distraction in lessons as possible, to test a teacher's patience, to bend the school rules to find their breaking point. And to utterly stress test the system. All without getting sanctioned. It's the role of every secondary school boy.

Really, gentlemen? I sense some of you are frowning, perhaps saying to yourselves. "Why do I want to disrupt lessons? I liked my teachers at my old school, I liked learning. Won't learning help me in later life with my further education, with my future jobs?"

As this Summer Skool course goes on, we hope to convince you that the most important thing in school life is to be free to explore and investigate your interests, make your own discoveries, develop your character in your own way, recognise the things that you feel motivated to learn, and to be creative. Having a laugh, having good mates, like-minded, fun-seeking friends. That's what it's all about. But secondary school these days doesn't give you much choice; it's all about what they want to force onto you. Secondary education is an imposition. Secondary education should be secondary.

OK, I know, some of you really do want to be *class boffins*, to show off how clever you are, to impress one or two teachers. That's fine, gentlemen. Really! I really mean it. You boffins too will have an important part to play in our mission.

Work hard. Learn a lot. Get good exam grades. Listen to your teachers. And make the most of your opportunities. This is the kind of propaganda that governments, education authorities, school heads, and classroom teachers have been telling pupils and your parents for years. Why? It's in their interests. That's why. They get paid good money to extend this myth. They'll even encourage you to try harder so that you can go to university to develop yourself academically. And then you'll be able to become… what… just like them. Academics. It's outrageous! Academic courses bear little relation to real life. They are well, merely academic! In the Oxford Dictionary (another book that many of you will never need) the word *academic* is defined as *abstract, too much enslaved to principles,*

impractical. So you see, even the Oxford academics recognise that being academic is a waste of space. Academic ideas were started by people like Socrates and Plato thousands of years ago – what did they know about life? They didn't even have iPads.

A preposterous load of irrelevance. Look at the evidence. Tell me when in the last month has anyone outside school asked you to quote Shakespeare, work out simultaneous equations, discuss the reasons the Romans invaded Gaul? (Or was it the other way round? Doesn't matter.) Yet these will be exactly the types of topics you'll come across at your secondary school. How boring is that? Not just boring, but pointless.

Now look at some of the things you'd really like to know. How to get past Level 7 on Carbuster Three. How to text five people at once using only your nose. How to download *Miley Cyrus's* latest video on your G5 mobile. How to kick or throw a ball wicket-to-wicket, drive a car even faster, parkour across rooftops, freefall from an orbiting hot air balloon; the list is endless. But bet you you'll hardly ever come across any of these over the next five years at your new improved state-of-the-art secondary school.

Instead they choose to teach the same old, boring stuff like how many sheep there are in the Czech Republic or the formulae for methylethylbenzoicfutile. Harsh! They even go so far as to set school rules to stop you texting your mates, wearing headphones, throwing a ball across the classroom. How outrageous is that?

Teaching a class is very different
to teaching a subject.

At primary school it was all a bit different. There your teacher knew she was there to teach a class. At secondary school most new teachers think they're there to teach a subject. What can they be thinking of?

You know my argument makes sense. Of course it does! Now as I look around the room I begin to see even the boffins starting to nod in agreement. You boffins will be the ones with a special role to play. Our crack troops. We'll even encourage you to work in class a bit harder than the rest – as that's your natural inclination. No, not to please the teachers, but conversely to help us in our mission.

Huh, I said "a bit harder", stop looking so pleased with yourselves, boffins. Don't get too carried away. Finally, gentlemen, I'm now going to introduce you to the man over there in the smart uniform; he's an ex-military man who I'm sure you'll warm to.

CLATTER AS BOYS TURN AROUND.

Major General Cuthbert-Butterworth will take you through what's expected of you at secondary school. He will introduce you to your Mission.

SMART FOOTSTEPS FROM THE BACK OF ROOM,
CULMINATING IN A SHARP DOUBLE STAMP.

THE MISSION.

Thank you, VP. Good-day, men. Cuthbert-Butterworth here. 27 years in The Royal Guards. Seen action in… huh… well, everywhere. Must keep this brief.

How many of you like a challenge? We're men. We all do. But taking on a challenge without proper direction, huh? Not knowing where we are going. No, that's like turning up on parade in a disorderly fashion with the wrong kit, huh? No way to approach anything. We

Seen action… well everywhere.

need to push together. Same tactics. Same direction. That's what we are here to learn, right? Same direction. Nothing less.

I'm here to talk to you about our mission… your mission for the next five or six years. The Mission! I'll keep this short. When one powerful country occupies another, what can the conquered people do, eh? They could succumb to misery and slavery, that's what. Misery and slavery.

Or they can resist! Great soldiers aren't just brave. They're smart. They don't line up against all-powerful odds with no hardware to match them. Blundering bogmyrtle, that'd be just plain stupid. No way to approach anything.

No, they take the subversive approach. They appear to

accept the new regime, then undermine it at every level they can. With clever diversion tactics. The most effective soldiers slow down the enemy's progress; they get them doubting why they are there; they stress-test the enemy's presence until everything breaks down. Nothing less, huh? If the enemy occupies your space; you occupy their minds. Only then will the powerful withdraw, leaving the once repressed people to get on with what they prefer to do.

Classrooms are occupied territories. Boys supposedly have little power. Over parents. Over teachers. That's utter balderdash and bogweed. In practice, things aren't as they first seem. Take teachers – there are usually 30 of us to every one of them. And they aren't expecting the deviousness of our insurgency.

Work hard, on irrelevant subjects. No way! No need. Just slow down the process to a standstill, get their troops – the teachers – to doubt their own backup systems, and just like anyone in an occupied country, at every opportunity you must stress-test their presence.

Keeping it short, I've split our mission into three parts. Just three things to remember. NOW! Sit to attention, men. ATTENTION! No, don't stand up. Sit! Listen well. These next two minutes are crucial.

The first part of your mission will be to address the pace of lessons, adopt tactics that will slow down the teaching. The more time the teacher is distracted, the less time the teacher has to teach, the less time you will be forced to learn. Assess the situation. Cut teaching time by just 12 minutes in each one-hour class; equivalent to one hour per day, nearly one day per week. Bung-O! That cuts down the next five years to only four. And we haven't started yet, huh? Result!

Getting the people occupying your world – the teachers – to

doubt themselves is more subtle. The second part of our mission is to occupy their minds. Make them question their own abilities.

Then one final push to victory. We stress test the school system. Here, you'll make the teachers' workload so great that they will eventually crack and crumble under the strain. We call them the 3Ss of the Mission: SLOW, SELF-DOUBT, STRESS! Memorise them, men.

OUR MISSION
1. **Slow Down the Lesson**
2. **Self-Doubt. Introduce it**
3. **Stress test the System**

Expect nothing less. Nothing Less. No one wants to succumb to things that are boring and pointless, just for the sake of filling time. Mithering marshmoss. That's no way to approach anything. Yet that is what the education system in this country has set out for you. Governments, academics and Senior Teachers have devised a cudweed of a curriculum. To enslave you, get you all tangled up. Utter bindweed! Nothing less.

INDISTINGUISHABLE MURMURING.

Today, I'm recruiting the next generation of Mission Musketeers. Put your hands up if you are in. All in? No? What's wrong with you there? Good-o! Settled.

Time to reward you with a break. In orderly fashion **Squad Stand**. Ready. Follow the boy at the front through the door. Slow march. Muster back here in 20 minutes. You there, don't shove. Don't break ranks yet. YOU! To the back, NOW! Pushing like that. Slithering slimeweed! No way to approach anything.

You have a mission. So too does the school.

Welcome back from break, gentlemen. Major General Cuthbert-Butterworth thinks you have the makings of a fine squad and are now ready for the next session. He'll be back with one or two more words of wisdom throughout the week.

Now, break over. Is everyone refreshed? Hope you enjoyed the sticky drinks and messy cakes. Still chewing over there? This week I must ask you NOT to bring any food into the classroom. Just put it there in the basket. But that's only this week. Once you start your new school, U-C-F-I, Undercover Classroom Food Infiltration is to be encouraged. Better still is sharing food around during lessons, particularly if you can throw it to, or maybe at, someone.

Silence now, please. Let's get on and learn a bit about what you will have to deal with from next September – school policies, behaviour management techniques and lots of school rules. In a nutshell, it's our mission to kick against the irrelevant, boring, pointless education system. But unsurprisingly we're not the only ones with a mission. Schools have one too. Their goals are despicable. Here are some of them:

- To keep children occupied and out of the way of adults during daylight hours.
- To tire boys out so that you'll rush around less.
- To keep you following useless rules for no apparent reason.
- To look down on you, to make you feel small.

- To interfere with your social life; to restrict the amount of time you have to chat and play with friends.
- To undermine your confidence, perhaps by embarrassing you with difficult questions in front of your friends.
- To foist all of this unnecessary learning onto you, the more seemingly useless the subject the better.
- To make you just like them. Academic.

That's it, gentlemen. Their mission. What the government, education authorities and schools want. Simple as that. So how do they go about it? They get teachers to do the dirty work, that's how.

Now, what I'm next going to tell you may come as a surprise. You probably won't have heard about this, not from any adults, certainly not from your teachers. I'll whisper this: teachers go to university to learn special tactics to keep you down.

I'll repeat that: **Teachers are taught special tactics to keep you down;** special tactics to make sure YOU behave in a way they want you to do. All of you. No exceptions. Utterly preposterous. You're looking shocked, gentlemen. Well here's another shocker. Look out for it. After all the pupils have gone home, teachers go to special behaviour lessons to discuss you and your mates. Yes, YOU specifically, and him. How to keep boys under their complete control. Bet you didn't know that. Why do you think that their cars are still in the car park as your bus pulls out?

And, there's something more. You've heard about INSET days. What do you really think they are for? To give you an extra day off? No way. Most INSET days are there to remind teachers how best to deal with you. They work on their tactics. They even have special websites and a newspaper for teachers, packed full of ideas about the way you children think and how to stop you from playing around in class. *The Times Educational Supplement.* Comes out every week. EVERY WEEK. They just won't let up. It's outrageous! Shake your heads all you like. This is what we are up against.

Every school, including yours will have Behaviour Policies – policies aimed mainly at altering YOUR behaviour. Disgraceful! What's so wrong with the way you behave, you might ask? Actually, gentlemen, and I'm sure by now you've noticed, different groups behave in different ways. Parents behave one way, grannies another, younger sisters another, older sisters (they can be quite odd) yet another. Boys want to behave like boys. They don't seem to understand that boys behave the way boys behave, full stop, not like their teachers and parents. I've got here in my hand a typical school document entitled *Behaviour Management Strategies*; I won't tell you where I got it, probably from YOUR new school. Even before you set foot in the new school, they will ask your parents to sign a School-Parent Agreement giving the school the power to discipline you with detentions, to isolate you, to take up your spare evenings with homework. Lots and lots of homework. After a seven-hour day in a sweaty classroom. Homework? Unspeakable! Once signed up, you'll be faced with all sorts of orders, from what to wear, what you can eat, which side of a corridor to walk down, to where you can talk and to whom you can speak. Some schools will even get your parents to agree that you can't bring in fun things, like music players, shock-pens, VITAs and even essentials like gum.

They are asking your parents to sign your life away. And most parents do, 'cause they have been conned by the education system into thinking that although they weren't brilliant at school, YOU can be. So long as you follow a few rules.

Then there are something called sanctions and rewards.

Sanctions cover things like detentions, staying in during playtime, litter picking – things to deliberately upset boys – and rewards such as stars, stickers, badges, merit certificates – again things to deliberately upset boys. And worst of all, when they give you a reward, to further embarrass you, they'll probably make you stand up in front of everyone in the school and shake hands with the Head.

You'll notice it as soon as you start secondary school, on your very first day. There on the walls will be all sorts of rules like "Be punctual", "Have the right equipment", "Hands up to speak", "No mobile phones", "Bags under desks" – then when you try to sit down next to your best mate, they'll tell you there's a special seating plan and move you to the other side of the classroom. Disgraceful!

And it's not just all the mentally taxing stuff, like French and literature and past participles that you'll be faced with. Woe betide you if you're little. You're really in for it. You'll see it in every secondary school. The new Year 7 pupils, particularly the smallest, skinniest boys are made to carry the biggest, heaviest rucksacks. It's a scandal!

These behaviour courses for teachers also cover specific tactics such as effective eye contact, how to gesture at you, never to smile until after Christmas (and they expect you to give them a present). These are powerful tactics, designed by eminent university professors and school managers. Schools believe that when it comes to you and them, they should have all the power. You need to know that, before you start. We are in an almighty power struggle and we can't afford to let them win.

It's outrageous. In EVERY school, the smallest, skinniest boys are made to carry the biggest, heaviest rucksacks.

TEACHERS – WHAT REALLY MAKES THEM TICK?

OK we've mentioned the outrageous and depressing education policies you'll face at secondary school. But you won't be dealing with systems. You'll deal with people – more precisely teachers. Teachers; they come in all shapes, sizes, and colours. But they are basically the same. They are usually well meaning. They start off seeming to like you and wanting to help you, to pass on their knowledge. But the fact that their knowledge is of little relevance to you seems to be beyond many of them.

Even when something might seem a bit useful, they mess up. For example in Maths lessons they could cover cool things like the time you've got when you free-fall from a plane or the optimum speed for a double somersault and twist in the skate park. But teachers just won't stop there. They have to go on to show you algebra.

All teachers believe that everyone should be interested in their subject, but most teachers show no real interest in another teacher's subject. Just observe the other teachers. Not many RE or History teachers are interested in inorganic chemistry. So why should YOU be? Totally hypocritical.

Your ordinary classroom teacher doesn't usually have any control over school rules, the curriculum, nor the education system's mission. Those things come from the top. Unfortunately, perhaps unwittingly, classroom teachers, by buying into the academic myth have become the frontline troops for the education system. No matter how pleasant they seem, they are tasked to implement the system. Teachers will present you with your primary objective.

Everyone keeping up? Well done, gentlemen. You've waited patiently. Now, let's get you involved. Let's see. At primary school did you acquire any misconceptions of how powerful teachers really are? Raise your hand if you can give me a few words to describe what you think secondary teachers will be like. You over there, go first.

Well nasty… 'av a go at us.

OK, I see you are playing for laughs. I don't want to discourage that, but let's try someone who wants to take this more seriously. Has anyone noticed that there is another adult in the room this lesson? Over there in the corner is Mr Godfrey – he's a typical teacher. Don't hide away. Come to the front, Mr Godfrey. Now, gentlemen. Give me some words to describe him. You, in the blue shirt.

Stern. Knows what he wants. Could be harsh, Sir.

Good. That's better. What do you think he will want to do when you go into his classroom? Not you again. Let's try the two people at the back. You… and you.

Give us lots of work, Sir.
Make us stay in if we misbehave.

Can we be more positive, gentlemen? What's his main purpose? It's not a trick question. What does a teacher think he's there for?

To… urgh… teach us?

Yes, of course. What else? To teach you. Although he'd probably turn that around and say that he would be there to help YOU to learn. Wouldn't you Mr Godfrey? He's nodding… and smiling. He's not so stern anymore, is he?

Help us... with things.

Go on, expand that thought. Help with what? You... then you, and you.

Help us with numeracy and literacy, to get... urgh... things right, Sir.
And history and geography.
And making things, Sir.
And RE and sport.
Sport's fun. Doesn't count. [FROM BACK]

Please don't butt in! Only answer when I indicate; though I must agree that some subjects at primary school are more like fun. And these indeed include Sport... and Art... and using computers and doing experiments. But secondary schools make even fun subjects seem quite boring. They give them boring names like Physics, and Design Technology and ICT. Even playing with messy, sticky things like lovely, gooey dough is called Food Technology.

So, how can your teacher make life difficult if you boys prefer to do something other than learn during a lesson? You, first... Give me your Top Ten. I'll write these on the board.

GIVE US DETENTIONS
POINT STRAIGHT AT US
SHOUT
SEND US OUT OF THE ROOM
PUT US ON REPORT
SEND US TO THE HEAD
PHONE OUR PARENTS
ASK OUR PARENTS TO COME IN
EXCLUDE US

That's only nine, but I guess someone will come up with another. And do you like these happening to you? No? Yet, gentlemen, day after day you'll be subjected to hours and hours of work, even more hours of homework and if you try to object they'll hit you with sanctions.

When you first come across teachers, you might think that they are all knowing, all powerful, calm and in control. This misconception is quite understandable, as most teachers are usually bigger than the average 11 year old. But, who really holds the power in the classroom? Gentlemen, YOU do! Masterful teachers, towering over you with their clever schemes won't last forever; if you are in any doubt you only have to think ahead. In the next five years even the biggest of teachers will shrink before your very eyes. By Year 10, they'll seem smaller, fatter, greyer, more hunched up and more cautious of you. So you may as well learn this at the start and adopt tactics sooner rather than later. It's a fact of life. Teachers only look bigger; it doesn't last.

Teachers only look bigger (especially to Year 7s)

Having said all of that, many a Year 7 pupil has been conned for a term or two. It's quite understandable. But don't worry, while the College Professors think they have been really clever devising behaviour tactics for teachers to use, the tactics rarely work fully in real life. It's academic, nothing more. And remember what we said about things that are academic. Little to do with real life.

Now I hear you saying, gentlemen, if schools have all those behaviour management systems, won't the school leaders use the school's behaviour policy to support any teacher in difficulties? Won't it be easy for teachers to report you? You'd think so. But it doesn't happen often. Inexperienced classroom teachers start off really keen and spend ages writing behaviour reports, concerning themselves with the details of what you've done. But who are these reports for and who has the time to read them on a daily basis? Senior teachers have no time for such detail; they'll give them no more than a quick glance. So little or nothing happens. Support for a teacher struggling with behaviour is usually no more than a few encouraging phrases, such as "sort it out yourself". Any new teacher who doesn't want to appear too inept, will pretty soon keep his reports about you to a bare minimum.

Let's get back to your list. Consider what's on the board, here. Do any of these hurt? Really? Do they actually physically hurt? No. So no harm done. Mr Godfrey can't hit you. Nowadays, he can't even tweak your ear. The MOST Mr Godfrey can do is to ask the Head to exclude you, and what does that do. It gives you extra days off school. No problem. Treat them like extra holidays.

In reality Mr Godfrey is likely to do very little. Time isn't on his side. He's too busy to do much about your challenges. Not when he has to cope with the 40 or more Mission tactics we've got for you this week, designed specifically to help you with the 3Ss while discouraging teachers from applying behaviour policies. To whet your appetites, we'll start next lesson with four or five TACTIC TASTERS. Quick break, then we'll be back with some real action. Ten minutes.

STOP! Don't get up yet. Now, you may leave. Row nearest the window first. Good, orderly. Very orderly. Remember, only 10 minutes.

A Taste of the Week's Tactics.

Welcome back, gentlemen. Over the years, we've found that boys become fully engaged… Gentlemen, GENTLEMEN, please. Break is over. We've found that boys only become fully engaged when they understand where a lesson is taking them. So what's ahead? Lots of tactics, that's what. You'll learn dozens throughout the rest of the week. But to begin, we've five fairly basic tactics; the more subtle ones start tomorrow. Can anyone tell me what was the Major General's first S of his 3Ss? Yes, you, jumping up and down on the front row.

Sir, Sir. Somethin' like slowin' things down, like.

Excellent! So, this morning's tasters will be about slowing down the start of your lesson before the teacher can get going. Real classics for you.

Everyone, start to imagine. NOW! Imagine you're all in the classroom. Teacher has the learning outcome on the board. She's closed the door. She's asked someone to hand out the books. All seems orderly. If this goes on too long, she'll have you working hard and learning something useless, like how to make sacks out of flax.

Your mission is to turn order into chaotic bewilderment. Remember, the later the lesson begins, the less work you'll have to do. As soon as she is about to explain what's on the board and get work underway, you need to somehow break it up. Your first move must involve a reasonable request; the more boys involved the better. Reasonable interruptions might include:

"Miss, I have no book.
"Sir, I have no pen."
"Miss, my book's full."

Always say "Miss" or "Sir". It'll make your request seem polite, and she can't sanction you for doing what you couldn't possibly consider to be bad. Everyone. Notebooks ready? Copy these down.

Tactic One– Involve your teacher in idle conversation.

Let's start by being friendly. If you can engage teachers in a friendly conversation before they even get going, then the less time there'll be for the main lesson, the less time you'll have to work. For boys, this is best tried with male teachers. Just as he's about to introduce the lesson, ask him something he's interested in, like:

"What car you got, Sir?"
"What football team you support?"
"Did you ever play cricket, Sir?"
"Sir, is that a lumberjack hat you're wearing?"

If he doesn't answer, you might try turning around to the rest of the class and saying "bet he's got a Skoda" or "Scunthorpe United, hah". If this doesn't encourage him to put you right, then say "I support... We're the best". Then shut up. He is unlikely to sanction you for being proud of your team, but you've distracted everyone for a minute or so. Now the rest can join in a noisy "Chelseeee", "Citeeee" or even "United! United!" Someone might shout out Saturday's results. Uproar. Just because someone asked a friendly question.

But if, gentlemen, your teacher does start to talk cars or football then **bingo!** At least five minutes will pass without him even noticing the time. And if he's a new teacher, then don't forget to ask, "Sir, what's your name?" Then if he answers, mispronounce it, so that he will have to repeat it.

TACTIC TWO– INVOLVE YOUR TEACHER IN RELEVANT CONVERSATION.

This can be tried by anyone who wants to impress the teacher, and it takes less than a minute to prepare. Make sure you've written something in your books to do with a question, but it needn't be much, nor take up any real brainpower. Just as she's about to refer to the lesson objectives on the whiteboard, one or two boys should approach her desk with open exercise books. She'll have to stop the lesson for you. Try something like "Miss, yesterday I got stuck on Question 12a. Where am I going wrong?"

At worst she'll just send you back to your seats. Most teachers will at least glance at your question. Whatever, her train of thought will have been interrupted and she'll have to repeat the introduction to her topic. On average two minutes of the lesson lost.

But if she falls for it and starts to involve herself in your question, she'll probably take her eyes off the rest of the class. You

28

can bet some hothead will soon spot the opportunity and within seconds uproar could occur. Paper planes, bag snatching, general chatter. It might take four minutes to settle things down. Plus an extra two as you are still at the front and can ask about question 12a again.

You don't only have to use this tactic at the start of lessons. It can be used at any time of course. But the start is particularly effective. Getting the idea about tactics? Good. Now we can look at two real classics, used in every classroom, every day, in every school.

Tactic Three – the classic 'no pen' tactic.

What's this I'm holding up, gentlemen? Yes, it's a pen. One of the most basic classroom tactic tools. It can be used at the start of a lesson to slow things down, in the middle to break things up and for really disruptive tactics to start a chain reaction by goading other boys. Prod, prod.

Here's what you do. First, raise your hand slowly without speaking. Then after a minute or so, say quietly. "Sir, I have no pen". Again, note the use of "Sir". Always be polite. Few teachers fail to respond to a request for basic equipment. They'll either tell you off for not having one, or get into a conversation about where you've left it. As it's standard school policy that pupils equip themselves with the basics, always have a good explanation. It can take minutes off a lesson. Either way you've stopped the teacher from addressing the class and diverted everyone away from the topic.

If your teacher is canny enough to ignore you or to wave you aside, then go to a second level. Comments such as "I need one.

Otherwise I can't work" or "How do I do my work without a pen?" These often provoke a reaction.

Still no response from the teacher. Level three. Turn around and say to anyone nearby in as exasperated a way as you can "He won't lend me a pen". That person may even join in with "Sir, give him a pen". You've now started a joint tactic – a Combo – which we'll cover in greater detail on Wednesday.

The unresponsive teacher may now say "Borrow one from a friend".

You reply: "I have no friends". This always gets a laugh, rarely a detention. You could then rumble about in your friend's bag for a pen in such a way that he pulls back the bag. That's the start of what we call a *Commotion Combo*... again, more about them later.

Just by not having a pen at the start, gentlemen, you've delayed things by two or three minutes. Yet at no time have you seemed unreasonable and it's unlikely that the teacher will hit you with anything more than "bring one in tomorrow". Even if he says "bring one in tomorrow or I'll give you detention", no worries. By tomorrow, the teacher will have had to teach at least 100 other pupils and will most likely have forgotten your individual pen.

The subtle thing about the pen trick is that you need one to write. Without one you can't take part in the lesson, which *obviously, gentlemen*, you're keen to do. While EVERY school has a rule that EVERYONE must come fully equipped for EVERY lesson, the Pen Rule is the first rule Heads and the school leadership team ignore. I bet that if your teacher complains to his line manager that boys never seem to have pens or pencils, nine times out of 10 the reply will be "No pen. Easier to give them one. There are plenty in the cupboard".

Try it! It's one of the first signs that the school policies are breechable. It shows that although the Heads have set the rules, they don't think through how to enforce them. I've never known a boy not to end up with a pen who says "No pen, today, Sir".

Pens – the first sign that a school's rules can be broken.

Once you've been given a pen, keep it! Most teachers will let you keep it; after all you'll need to use it in later lessons. So don't give it back. But, as soon as the lesson is over, you'll need to lose it, otherwise you won't be able to use the pen tactic at the start of the next lesson. If you have to go outside to another building between lessons, drop it in a bush, or a waste bin or behind a wall. Most schools have hiding places. They've been designed that way. Caretakers are taught to look out for pens in the most unusual places. But if your school doesn't have any hiding places, or schedules lessons so that you remain in the same building all morning, then keep the pen until break-time and once in the playground stamp on it; probably why it's called *break* time. You can tell a school that organises its timetables to reduce pen hiding opportunities – the playgrounds are full of shattered plastic.

We'll come back to losing pens when we consider tactics for the middle of a lesson. But some days, you might want to keep and reuse the pen. Spitball days. What we used to call peashooters.

Tactic Four – the classic 'no exercise book' trick.

Exercise books. Finishing your book, not having a book, someone writing in your book – the teacher or another pupil – these are all good excuses to delay teaching.

Let's start with not having one. To your teacher, leaving your book at home is bad. She might be inclined to sanction you. However, taking your book home to do extra revision or homework is good. So when you say you have no book, you need to qualify it.

So don't say "Miss, I have no book", or "I can't find my book". Instead say "Miss, they (the book monitors) haven't given me my book", or, "Sir, I took my book home for revision and forgot that it's Week Two and that we have Geography today instead of tomorrow". Discussing your reasons for no book, gentlemen, seems reasonable. You'd be unlucky to be given a sanction for asking, but you've used up at least a minute; perhaps much more if you go over where it might be in your bedroom.

If you have your book with you but are within three pages of the end, ask for a new one. "Sir, my book's full." If the teacher says "No it isn't, you've still got three pages to go" then just answer "Yes, but you told us to leave room at the end for the special notes you give us". The irony of having to leave a space for instructions that haven't yet been given and won't ever be written in this book is beyond many teachers, especially men teachers, and you'll get a new book.

Other ways to get to the end of a book quickly, and therefore have a reason to interrupt, is to write in very large letters with lots of gaps or to leave blank pages. If a teacher ever questions these gaps, say that you had some worksheet or other to paste in but had no gluestick that day. Your teachers will be pleased that their worksheets are not being used as paper aeroplanes and will probably let it pass.

And, why should you have to write in a scruffy, thumbed and curled up book when someone's just got a new one? That would be outrageous. So up pipes the class swot with "Sir, I've finished my book. Can I have a new one?" The teacher checks the boy's book to see that it's full and then nearly always needs to take two minutes to fumble in a packet of books, often wrapped tightly in plastic and near impossible to separate. Two minutes gone. Now *"All for one, one for all"* is what we Mission Musketeers say. If one boy is given a new book, then anyone with just a few blank pages left might feel that they have the right to ask the teacher to check to see if they can have one too. You'll never get sanctioned for asking for something you need. But each boy should leave it a minute or two before their request. The teacher will be like a yoyo, going back and forth to check books.

Now, another type of book – your text books. Most secondary schools keep sets of books in each classroom. Maths books in Maths rooms. French books in MFL rooms. But some schools can't afford…

Don't interrupt, please. What? MFL stands for Modern Foreign Languages. That's most languages apart from Latin and Ancient Greek.

MURMUR.

What? What's Latin? It's a fine, old language used by Romans… *[PAUSE]* Ah I see, you're smiling, showing me that you're practising the art of interrupting. Slowus Interruptus.

But you've just wasted two minutes, not very clever when you've come here to learn. Quite unacceptable, WASN'T IT? I know it's satisfying to start to use a newly-learned tactic to see if it works, but NOT HERE, please. Wasting good time. We'll give you the opportunity later to go through your paces. BUT NOT NOW!

Let's get back to books. An organised teacher will appoint book monitors to hand out exercise books and text books at the start, while most of you are entering the room. Offering to be a monitor not only gets you in the teacher's good books – sorry, gentlemen, about the pun – but also it opens up lots of opportunities. No-one expects you to place the books carefully on each desk. So why not chuck the odd book, and just wait to see what happens? A second boy may fumble the book; then a third may join in with a distracting comment or two.

TACTIC FIVE – BORROW THE TEACHER'S TEXT BOOK.

Who's the bravest in this room? From your show of hands, half of you it seems. Well, this tactic is for a brave lad on the front row. Often front row pupils are boys just trying to please, boffins trying to get nearer the learning zone and naughty types made to sit at the front where the teacher can keep a closer eye on them. But sometimes they're mates, special agent types with smiley faces. More about them this afternoon.

This tactic works only because most schools (by that I mean Heads) are mean. They provide 16 textbooks per class. That's one for every two boys and a spare for the teacher. So while the teacher is scanning the back of the class, go under the radar and just borrow the textbook from his desk. Quite reasonable, he should know the subject, he doesn't really need it. But you do.

When he wants to refer to the next exercise, he'll find his book has gone. Observe what he does next. He'll look under his papers first, then on the window sill to see if he's left it there. It all takes a few minutes and allows a chatterbreak to develop. Then he'll look at YOU – the Braveheart. Be ready. Just say "Sorry, needed it, I'm on a different page to him (boy next to you)" and hand the book back.

You'll never get sanctioned for borrowing something that is helping you to learn, but it's taken another few minutes out of the lesson. A really strict teacher might take his frustration out on you by threatening a detention. Then the rest need to join in with a sympathetic "Sir, that's not fair. He was only working." The longer the discussion, the shorter the time left to teach. Also tomorrow we'll show you how the more pupils that get involved, the less likely you'll get a detention.

So that's our fifth opening tactic. A lot to take in this busy first morning, gentlemen, but it'll all be worthwhile come September. Well done, everyone. NO. DON'T GET UP YET. Let me finish. This afternoon we'll take a closer look at the different types of Mission Musketeer you might become. We'll be talking about you... and YOU... and even YOU.

NOW it's lunchtime. Turkey twislers and chips. Followed by Olympic Ring donuts. Colourful, five inches in diameter with double icing sugar. Oh, and our ever-popular pies-on-the-side. When you are ready! Nice and orderly, now. Front row first. Off you all go.

Clattering of seats. Background music starts. Sounds a bit like the Boomtown Rats and 'Tell me why I don't like Mondays', getting louder as the boys exit the room.

BARELY AUDIBLE OVER MUSIC AND CLATTER OF FOOTSTEPS.
Nothing more than the usual enthusiastic bunch, Godfrey, eh?

Boys will be boys. But, what type are you?

Let's start this afternoon by entering in an orderly fashion. No rushing, please, gentlemen.

CLATTERING... THEN SILENCE.

Just looking around the room today, I'd expect most of you to be regular, average pupils. Not too bad, but no way a goody-goody. During your time at secondary school, most of your fellow pupils will be like you. Nothing too extreme, but curious, wanting to try out new things, game for a bit of a laugh. Most of you are in the category we call *Mates*.

But boys aren't all the same. Other pupils may like to work on their own, as undercover operators so to speak. A few might not want to join in at all. But everyone WILL, willingly or unwittingly, one way or another, have a part to play in the Mission. As well as mates there will be four other types to look out for. Not as many boys fall into these categories, I admit, but it's worth knowing they are around and could be in your classroom. I'll write them on the board. These are the:

- **Hothead Attention-Seekers**
- **Silent Assassins**
- **Nerds and Boffins**

Let's start with the noisiest ones.

Hothead Attention-Seekers.

We've all come across them. They want to call out at every opportunity. They are often the first to try our tactics. But it's not because they are extra brave. More that they don't know how to be subtle. Nor polite. So they are the first to get detentions, to use bad language in front of teachers, to be removed from lessons, to argue with the Head of a Department. They are often excluded, hardly in class for long, and so are less useful to the rest of us when carrying out the Mission. But like Exocet missiles they can make a big bang at any time during a lesson. Don't condone them, gentlemen, but use the opportunities they present. They provide the best excuse possible to slow down a lesson. When they are sounding off the teacher can hardly expect you to concentrate. Your lack of work is far less important to her when she's got hothead Matty to contend with.

Sit back and enjoy the ride, gentlemen. Put your pen down and start chatting to your neighbour as if to say "what's going on?" At the end of the lesson, you might say quietly to the teacher "Didn't get a lot done today, Miss, what with Matty kicking off".

Silent Assassins.

Some boys delight in winding up the rest of you. A pretend winding up is a great Combo-tactic, but these guys are for real and they don't intend it as part of the Mission. It's just that they are anti-social and want to annoy not only the teacher but also everyone else in the class. These are the *Silent Assassins*. Unloved by everyone. They are resented by most boys because they rarely get caught and so get away with a disproportionate amount of mischief. Although their behaviour indirectly slows down lessons, and so helps the Mission, they can be a bit annoying. Get an elastic band fired at you, or suddenly find your ruler's been mysteriously snapped and you'll know what I mean.

They're not likeable, rarely get involved in the best joint attacks, and can hardly be called mates. But they're there and you'd best be aware. If you join in with them and are both caught, they'll find some way out of it. They'll diss you just like that. You'll get the wrap. They rarely will!

Nerds.

Sad, gentlemen. So sad… Some boys will just not get involved in the Mission. Don't ask me why. Early upbringing or something. What were their parents playing at?

They can be the awkward ones that prefer to sit quietly trying to concentrate on their work and they actually like teachers to like them, even though most teachers can't be fussed liking them. I don't know what's up with them. Talk about Mission tactics and they'll turn away. Always wanting to please adults, looking for recognition, some of them even brush their teeth during school break-time. They deserve everything they get. They are the *Nerds*.

Generally, nerds do little for the Mission. They of course benefit when you slow down a lesson, but they just won't contribute to the class's overall Mission effort. What can you do? What you mustn't do is to threaten or bully them, particularly outside classes. This will draw attention to yourself and may alert teachers to the fact that you are asking them to help with tactics. The one saving grace with nerds is that they can be so quiet that they are unlikely, unless provoked, to say anything to teachers about the Mission at all. They're just too withdrawn. They may snap out of it someday, but who wants to wait that long?

However hard we all try to persuade them, nerds will be nerds. Just plain nerdy! Anything to annoy a nerd can prove a useful ploy, like borrowing his ruler, thereby provoking a response and causing him to distract the teacher. Clever, eh? Nerds don't want to get involved in a slowing tactic, yet inadvertently the nerd does so by complaining. And again this helps the Mission because the teacher becomes confused – why should such a nice lad be playing up? Silent assassins are very good at winding them up.

And now for the Mission super troopers, the *Boffins*.

Boffins.

We referred to these guys earlier, gentlemen. Sometimes initially mistaken for nerds, but much more likeable. Boffins have the intelligence to devise new and exciting Mission tactics. Boffins like to test themselves, so they do more work than most pupils, ask more genuine questions (the ones teachers like) and can often even answer questions teachers get stuck on. But unlike nerds they are up for the Mission and as mentioned earlier can be our special agents. It's well worth cultivating a friendship with them – they might even help you with your homework.

When a boffin carries out a tactic, it can be ultra-effective. A teacher won't expect him to be deliberately slowing down a lesson; more likely he genuinely needs to interrupt because he needs help. Rarely caught out for punishment, boffins are the Special Services when it comes to prosecuting the Mission.

Other Special Agent Roles.

This isn't a new category, more a sub-category of mates. Some of you will have special advantages when it comes to carrying out tactics. Even if you're no boffin yourself, but if you are intelligent-looking (glasses help) or have a naturally smiley face… then there might be special agent roles for you. Teachers can't help smiling at boys with smiley faces. Mess with a teacher's computer, he'll know you are just having a laugh. Butt in, ask a daft question, others would get a detention. With smiley boys many teachers, in fact most people, just return the smile.

We can all practise to look attentive, engaged, quietly-spoken or innocent. It's worth studying the boys who are good at it; when reprimanded they look at the teacher, but slightly to one side, slightly down, never really up. Silent assassins are brilliant at this.

Of all the five categories, boffins are the closest to mates. Enjoy their company; they have the intelligence to get up to wheezes that no one else thinks of. Watch and be amazed.

Now, just for two minutes, I'd like you to reflect on the type of pupil you are or might want to become. And how you can play a part in the Mission. For you all WILL definitely have a part to play.

We'll round off our day with what teachers call a *Plenary*. Just a short time to summarise what you've learnt and for you to ask any questions.

RELATIVE QUIET.

PLENARY.

OK. Quick summary of the day, gentlemen. Schools want to put you down and they actually devise special ways to control your behaviour. Apart from our early tactics, this might seem a bit depressing. But today, you've heard the bad news. It's all good stuff tomorrow. So, while Mr Godfrey passes round Mars Bars to give you a boost, look at the whiteboard behind me. This is how YOU are going to turn the tide. Watch carefully. Very, very carefully.

CLICK!
HUSHED SILENCE WITH ONE OR TWO COUGHS (MOST PROBABLY TOO MUCH, CARAMEL, EATEN TOO QUICKLY.)

CLICK!
DISTINCT MURMURING.

CLICK!
INCREASINGLY LOUD MURMURINGS OF AGREEMENT.

CLICK
EXCITED MURMURINGS.

CLICK!
CHEERING.

CLICK!
CHEERING.

CLICK!
APPLAUSE

CLICK!
APPLAUSE, CHEERING, CLAPPING, STAMPING OF FEET.

CLICK!
SINGING… WE ARE THE CHAMPIONS.

WHISTLE. LOUD BLAST!
SILENCE.

Told you. Tomorrow, gentlemen, we start to take control. Now, thank you… QUIET! I still need just a few more minutes of your time for any questions.

STUNNED SILENCE.
AFTER A MINUTE OR TWO, WHICH SEEMS A LOT LONGER…

So, no questions, then, gentlemen? Speak up. Nice and loud, now. Nothing? There must be something you haven't quite understood, today. OK, I'll start to ask you some questions to see what you have learned on your first day at Sum…

Sir… Sir?

Good. Let's have it. Our first plenary question of the week. Baited breath. Make it a good one.

Certainly is, Sir.

OK. The first question. Can't wait. Is everyone ready for this? Fire away.

Sir, what's your name?

Most interesting. A most interesting question. We'll discuss this further when we talk more about tactics; I'd like all of you to remember his question – it gives you a powerful early tactic in carrying out the Mission. Any other questions? Yes, you. Speak up now.

Sir, what IS your name?

I'm known as The Vice Principal. Another question, please. Keep your questions to what we have covered today.

Is all learning right bad?

… Sir. Always say "Sir".

Is all learning bad, Sir? Mr Vice Principal, Sir.

Thank you. I didn't say all learning was bad. If I did, then I didn't mean learning; I meant irrelevant teaching.

On the contrary. Learning is ALWAYS good. Just think about it. People only learn what they want to learn; the rest they forget. We all have a natural curiosity to investigate things, to develop our interests. Learning how to play a new computer game or bend a ball into the goal. No problems there. Learning should always lead to fun. And fun should lead to learning. It's all those irrelevant facts that your schools want you to learn; that's what you need to be wary about.

But, Sir, Miss tells us that we wanna know the 3Rs to get on.

Miss tells you. Miss? Your teacher. Haven't we said that you can't trust teachers? They are working for the education system. Alright of course you have to read and write. How else would you know what's in the game console box? But really, there's only one R that matters. RESPECT. Respect from your fellow pupils. The better you carry out the Mission, the more respect you'll get. Forget the 3Rs – phuh, the 3Rs don't even all start with an R. The 3Ss are what's important.

Sir, if you get, like, a well good teacher, a really, really good one like. Then how do you stop her from telling you something that's interesting? Know what I mean? If she's interesting? Know what I mean, if the class are so interested that they want to listen and not interrupt... Sir?

Interesting teachers. It has been known that they exist. Engagers. We'll talk more about these tomorrow. They can be trouble. They make their lessons so interesting that pupils look forward to the lesson. When this happens there's a danger perhaps that the class will learn something irrelevant. I know what you mean. Their engaging teaching might undermine the Mission.

Yes, Sir, that's what I mean.

OK, let me tell you what WE mean. You wouldn't want a teacher who is always doing interesting things to spoil it for the rest. But most teachers only have the odd interesting lesson in them each term anyway. Most of the time they are too tired. This might sound contradictory, but if most of you want to hear a particular teacher or a particular lesson, then what I say is go along with it. Keep the Mission tactics for the NEXT lesson.

I once knew an English teacher who came up with the most interesting lesson ever devised on *Waiting for Godot*. He was so proud of it that he kept it back for Ofsted. But Ofsted didn't come that year. Nor the next. By the time they did, they'd changed the set book to *Mice and Men*.

Sir. Don't goin' along with lessons kinda spoil the Mission? Beyond good, that, Sir.

Not necessarily. It's one of those odd things. If some teachers give interesting classes and you are engaged most of the time in their lessons, this soon becomes common knowledge among other teachers that don't get much attention. This affects the really conscientious, new teachers who just wonder what they are doing wrong. They take advice from the Engagers. They try again and again. And fail. If a few successful teachers (more about them tomorrow) are successful, this can only undermine the confidence of the rest.

Before we leave the question, though, if a normally boring teacher ever comes up with an interesting lesson, then get involved. They'll come out of the lesson thinking that they've got something right at last, only next lesson to have the rug pulled out from under them. Sporadic engagement adds to their bemusement and this leads to even more self-doubt.

If we slow down the lessons and make them more relaxing for us, won't that also help the teachers to relax? When we are supposed to stress them out... Sir?

What an excellent question. Are you a boffin, boy? A good bit of logic, there. And well expressed. Well done. In practice, it rarely happens. Teachers are programmed to get you involved, to get things moving forward. When pupils relax, and don't seem inclined to work at pace, teachers are made to work doubly hard. If you are particularly slow and seem not to understand, then you are making them doubt their own teaching abilities, which causes them even more stress. It's a double-whammy – two parts of the Mission accomplished at once. Self-doubt and stress!

Don't get it, Sir. Won't we get booted out if we keep slowin' things down?

OK. You might get expelled if you do something really bad, like hit someone. But slowing down a lesson by two minutes here, two minutes there. No way. Teachers expect that kind of thing. They don't like it. But schools tolerate it. They even have a phrase for it, *low-level disruption*. Teachers discuss it; many Heads dismiss it. Some Heads can't believe it takes place.

No-one in my experience has ever been thrown out for low level tactics. The odd pupil might do something bad, really bad on the one occasion, and he's out. But low level distraction rarely gets that reaction from the school. Low level – that's all the Mission asks for.

Not even if we go on and on? Urgh, Sir?

Remember that no-one is asking you to work alone on Mission tactics or for a single boy to interrupt continuously throughout the whole lesson. There are 30 of you. Share the responsibilities. He slows things for a minute here; you for a minute there. Then the next boy. Soon half the lesson's gone and no-one has done enough individually to get even a slight reprimand. Yet collectively you've achieved a lot. And when the teacher reflects on his lesson, how much time has been lost and how little you've done today, then he'll start to doubt his abilities. Mission accomplished.

Nearly time to go home. You're looking a little jaded now. So I'll end the questions there. Let's just reflect on what we have learnt today.

Isolate us, Sir. Sir, isolate us.

Eh? No interrupting over there?

Tenth thing. Sir. Isolate…

QUIET! Just go and stand by the wall. NOW! I want you all to reflect on what we have learnt today. Secondary education should be secondary to exploring what we are interested in, being ourselves and having fun with our mates. Schools use tactics to make us learn facts and behave in unnatural ways. And we've shown you that a lot of teachers want us to grow up to become academic, just like them.

But there are ways to counter this; every boy at secondary school can help by playing his part in our three-fold Mission. Remember there are three Ss in MiSSSion! Here they are again, something to think about as you leave.

1. **Slow Down the Lesson**
2. **Introduce Self-Doubt**
3. **Stress Test the Teacher**

Gentlemen, that's it. I hope you've had an interesting first day. Some of you may still be wondering what you've got yourselves into. But don't worry. We've spoken a little about what makes your ordinary classroom teachers tick. Tomorrow we'll look at the best ways to wind them up and we'll show you that a wound-up teacher hardly ticks like a precision timepiece – more like a ticking time bomb. Tomorrow we'll start to show you how to make them explode. You may start to pack up now.

RIGHT, gentlemen. Stand, please. One last note of caution. At home tonight, be very discrete. No-one, particularly your parents and teachers, should suspect that you are here. Ready, orderly fashion now.

As they march out, Pink Floyd's 'Another Brick in the Wall' plays gently in the background, rising to a crescendo with the boys heartily joining in to 'Hey teachers, leave them kids alone'.

IN LOW VOICE.
See Godfrey. They're a good bunch. Doubts? What doubts?

Day Two

In a teacher's typical day there's little time for sanctions. The boys learn to play by the rules. A lesson in Teacher Misconceptions and Differentiation. Mystery of the feathers solved.

TUESDAY, LESSON 1
Why teachers have no time to discipline you.

CLATTER, CHATTER, SHUFFLING.

Thank you. Thank you. Settle in now. It's Day Two, gentlemen. Such a nice sunny day out there. Welcome back. Most of you seem to be here. One or two missing, perhaps? What's that, Godfrey? We seem to have them all except seven. I can confidently predict that they'll be back; once they've heard about today. This, gentlemen, is the day Summer Skool takes off.

Just now some of you did seem to be drifting in, chatting, not really ready for the next gripping instalment. This gives me a good point on which to start. Now, a typical school allows boys to be one or two minutes late to a lesson. After all it can take two minutes for 30 children to walk through the door. So legitimately you can be two minutes late. But teachers can't be even two seconds late. They must be there at the classroom door when you arrive. Ready to start their lesson. With lots of books and things for you to do. Ever thought how they manage to do this?

A TEACHER'S TYPICAL DAY

Step forward, Mr Godfrey, again. Now, gentlemen, please be quiet while I tell you not only about how Mr Godfrey manages to be always there for his lessons, but all the other things he has to have ready in a typical teacher's day[1]. YOUR teacher will have a day much like Mr Godfrey's. To teach at secondary school, Mr Godfrey will probably wake up at 5.45 am and be up and about at around 6.15 in the morning.

[Dear Reader, in going into the details of a typical teacher's day, the next few pages have become crammed with tightly printed text. If reading this looks a bit daunting, then just skip these paragraphs and start again at 3.20pm. A mere glance should tell you that a teacher's day is intense with little time to relax. Oh, go on, then, read it all, but quickly. Do what many teachers do: flick and tick!]

7AM
Mr Godfrey travels for 45 minutes or more, in rush-hour traffic jams to get to school between 7.45am and 8am.

7.45AM
Mr Godfrey will enter his classroom and try to open his emails, not that he really wants to as new emails usually lead to extra work. The school IT system may take a long time to boot up as it uploads all the new software that has mysteriously appeared overnight. He will then check his interactive whiteboard; its calibration always seems to go awry overnight. He will nod to one or two departmental colleagues as they pass by outside his

classroom, but they too are in a hurry. They will rarely engage in stimulating conversation; they just don't have the time.

8.10AM
Mr Godfrey proceeds to the Staffroom. Often he goes there to photocopy worksheets for his lessons. Teachers' Unions don't like teachers to photocopy, but it's quicker to do it himself and he knows which page goes where. Also he goes there to read the noticeboards. He'll look in his in-tray for specific messages, again many with requests to do things he hadn't planned for. Around 8.20 he and his fellow teachers may have a Staff Meeting, either with his head of department, or at least once a week with the Head Teacher. Believe it or not he likes these meetings, as it is the one part of the day when he doesn't have to think; he can sit back and listen. But such meetings only last a few minutes, and often he comes away with another three unexpected things to do.

8.40AM
Mr Godfrey returns quickly to his classroom. Clammer! It's full of people already – his Form Group of 20 pupils. He goes back onto his computer, registers them, sorts through and hands out lots of messages, some very general, others specific to individual pupils. Then they all scuttle away to their first lessons. Now the real day begins.

9AM
Mr Godfrey's first lesson on his subject. Typically, 30 pupils will enter the room. Most likely he'll be standing by his desk. The desk may look fairly haphazard with piles of papers, exercise books, lost ties, but Mr Godfrey thinks he knows where everything is. After all

it's only Lesson One. He'll have the lesson objectives on the board ready for his pupils to copy down, while he uploads the register. During the next few minutes he has to settle his pupils down, keep them all interested and engaged, introduce the new topic they'll be learning, hand out worksheets and other resources, ask questions and answer questions… all the time scanning the room to see what they are all up to, who's on task and who's misbehaving. He must remember to hand out the correct textbooks, register the pupils for the lesson, check that last night's homework has been done, and give them tonight's homework. Follow their progress, each and every one of them. All 30 boys. It's expected of every teacher by the school authorities. Expected, but of course it's impossible. During a one-hour lesson mathematically a teacher has only two minutes for each of 30 pupils. In practice it's hardly 30 seconds. At the end of the lesson he has to see them all out of the room in an orderly fashion, while answering questions from keener pupils, collecting in resources and storing the fruits of their endeavours in a place he might recall at 4pm.

10AM

Lesson 1 is over. Now, can he relax? Just for two minutes? Not at all. He must find the notes for his second lesson. Unearth the resources, photocopies and relevant bits of string from the large pile on his desk. He must again fiddle with his computer to find the PowerPoint for the new lesson. He needs to find the new books. He needs to switch his mind from say a Year 7 basic lesson to a Year 10 GCSE class; from a quiet attentive group to a rowdy bunch. Then the hour-long process of meeting and greeting new faces, registering, engaging, teaching, sorting homeworks, sorting behaviour, sorting problems… starts again.

11AM

After two lessons, Mr Godfrey gets a break, usually 20 minutes but in some schools just 15. Or does he? The 20-minute break becomes 15 minutes as he deals with Lesson 2 boys with specific questions on today's topic, also boys who need to return rulers and colouring pencils etc etc. No time to relax; he has Period 3 in mind. Does he dash to the main office for more photocopies? Or go for a quick tea break? He shoos away any dawdlers, finds his classroom key from a ring full of similar keys, and attempts to lock his room with one hand, balancing books in the other.

11.08AM

He hurries down the corridor to the small departmental staff-office, where he hot-desks with two other teachers; he rumbles about the piles on this desk to find his resources, as opposed to theirs, the exercise books he marked last night, spare rulers, more pieces of string and whatever is needed for Period 3.

11.12AM

Someone offers him tea, which he accepts, plus cakes (all departmental teacher rooms are full of cakes and biscuits), and these he tries to consume in a dignified way while collecting his books with the other hand, all the time playing musical chairs with the other teachers as he tries to sit down for his hot drink. Most days he gives up, pours a bit down the sink, refills with cold water and then stands by the window. Gazing out, it seems far less hectic out there – more warm and sunny.

11.16AM

Mr Godfrey prepares to return to his classroom for Lesson 3. He could carry the tea back to his classroom, hoping the Head doesn't see him breaching health and safety rule 27ii on hot drinks in busy corridors. Better not, as could be a bad example to boys who have been told no drinks in the classroom. Better leave it on the window sill. Does he have time for the loo? No, and anyway it's being used.

11.18AM

Approach classroom, shimmying left and right to avoid any contact with a river of junior humanity. His doorway blocked by keen pupils early to the lesson, he struggles to find the key to unlock the classroom door.

11.20AM

Period 3. This is his favourite class (all teachers have favourite groups, despite every child *mattering* equally). But it's just as busy as Lessons 1 and 2. Fiddling with his computer. Meeting and greeting. Checking the interactive whiteboard. Registering. Replacing Year 10 books with Year 9 books (no wonder books get mixed up). Checking homeworks. Explaining this, explaining that.

12.20PM

His morning's work is over. No it's not. He still has a group of pupils hanging around his desk with extra questions (he doesn't mind as these are the good guys, wanting to learn). While answering their questions he must find somewhere safe for the homework books he's collected in, make sure the textbooks are back in the right place, rearrange the pile of books (and string) for the afternoon and… and wait for the boys attending lunchtime detentions. 12.20pm becomes 12.30pm by the time the detention boys arrive ("had to come from art, brushes needed washing"). At

12.40pm he can let them go. Oh no, here's another. This boy had a note to defer his detention by 20 minutes as he needs to have his lunch at the early sitting for some obscure dietary reason. So the 12.20pm teacher's lunchbreak now starts around a quarter to one.

12.45PM
Mr Godfrey finally locks his door on the morning, proceeds to the canteen for lunch, a four minute walk away, queues for five minutes, eats for five minutes, then into the main Staffroom to photocopy stuff for afternoon classes, looks for more messages, checks and answers any new emails.

1.10PM
The lunch *hour* is effectively over. Time flies when you're teaching. Back to his departmental hot desk. Find resources, exercise books, string for the afternoon. That cold cup of tea is still on the windowsill. More cake, perhaps.

1.18PM
Back to the classroom. Wade through a mass of boys queuing early outside his classroom. Unlock door at 1.19pm. Ready for Lesson 4 at 1.20pm. Now… what is it he has to teach this lot? He's beginning to have to think hard as confusion is starting to take hold. Oh, yes. Sort out the next lesson on his computer. Switch on the interactive whiteboard.

1.20PM
Meet and greet. Register. Hand out exercise books. Oversee handing out of textbooks. Engage brain for this topic. Manage teaching and learning for an hour. Manage behaviour. Manage homework. Close lesson. Answer extra questions from the good guys. Shoo out 30

boys. Meet and greet 30 more. Find Lesson 5 on his computer. Engage brain for next topic. Sort interactive whiteboard.

2.20PM
Meet and greet Class 5. Register. Hand out exercise books. Oversee handing out of textbooks. Manage teaching and learning for an hour. Manage behaviour. Manage homeworks. Close lesson. Answer extra questions from the good guys. Shoo out 30 boys.

3.20PM
Bell goes. Lessons over. Time to relax… NOT yet. Bus duty.

3.40PM
Back to the Staffroom. And a cup of tea, loo, relax. But not for long. He now needs to fit in all those extra unexpected tasks given to him today, answer more emails, return forms to the office, plan four or five lessons for tomorrow, start to mark those exercise books from today's five lessons. More photocopying. More emails. Behaviour log (some guy probably called Simms wants to know every little detail of bad behaviour).

4.30PM
Calls home to parents to sort out things like lost shoes, missing homeworks, poor behaviour, parents' evenings.

5.17PM
Not much marking done. Better leave for home. Load car with heavy-duty supermarket bag full of exercise books. An hour 15 minutes in heavy traffic. Stop for tomorrow's bread and milk. Home by 6.35pm. Cook and eat meal.

7.30PM

Mark more books (two classes of 30 books per night. This leaves only two minutes per book if he wishes to finish by 9.30pm).

9.30PM
Collapse.

10PM
Bed. Set alarm for just before 6am.

Phew!

Sorry. Haven't finished. That's in an easy week. There are daytime playground duties one day per week (another break gone); more departmental meetings; lunchtime catch-up classes or clubs, sort computer systems that stall or go down… the workload goes up and up. Atrocious!

Some weeks, gentlemen, Mr Godfrey has EXTRA, extra special duties. These include Professional Development meetings which can take two hours, Parent's Evenings for three hours, Prize Days, open evenings to impress prospective parents, plays and concerts… pupil subject reports, time-consuming end-of term assessment test marking (30 papers can take about five hours).

There's scarcely a week when something extra isn't needed. The result is that most teachers need Saturday mornings and Sunday afternoons just to keep up, leaving just half a day per week for Mr Godfrey to relax, do his gardening, or maybe watch his football team. The choice is his. And this goes on for seven or eight weeks with no let up.

Now teachers do have three or four *free* planning periods per week, but until recently they could be asked to cover the classes of other teachers who were away on courses or sick leave. Even nowadays these periods are hardly free for teachers to relax and eat cake. Instead there's more planning, marking and phone calls to parents. The conscientious teacher tries hard to fit in everything in their job description, but **it's impossible**. Think about it. A class of 30 that gets through a mere 10 questions in a lesson leaves the teacher with 300 questions to mark. Even if it takes only half a minute per question to correct and write comments, then that's two and a half hours for each class. In a one-hour free lesson? Impossible. That's what teachers' weekends are for. **Most new teachers can't do the job they are contracted to do in the time they are given to do it!**

I won't apologise for taking you through Mr Godfrey's day step by step, with hardly a break, gentlemen. You can see Mr Godfrey, here, wilting before your very eyes just thinking about his weekly tasks. What we are trying to put across is that teachers who do their jobs conscientiously, to the full, have little or no time for anything. Certainly not to discipline every pupil that deserves a detention. So teachers will be reluctant to give too many detentions, write behaviour reports, mark your work fully, or call your parents.

Relax. You do the relaxing.
Teachers never can.

They will be reluctant to send you out of the room – that wastes two or three minutes of a lesson. Tell the Head? They hardly have time to say "good day" to their Head let alone discuss your antics. Even good behaviour can add to a teacher's workload; more about that later. And as we'll show you later this week, even if they do give you a detention, you don't REALLY need to go to it.

I can see you're all exhausted just listening to what Mr Godfrey has to go through in a day. And by using our tactics, by following clear objectives and some underlying principles we can add to this workload. And to help me in our next lesson, who better…

FOOTSTEPS FROM REAR OF ROOM, SHARP STAMP CHEERING.

Don't know Godfrey; they just like him.

Underlying Mission Principles – the Magnificent Seven.

Steady men, steady. SILENCE!! Good. At ease, men. I'll get right into this. Let's keep it brief. First the Vice Principal needs to say something. Brief, VP, brief.

Yes, gentlemen. While the Major General and I are here together, we wanted to address a potential problem. Yesterday, gentlemen, we used a lot of military metaphors to get you engaged at the start of your course. From certain comments during break it would appear that some of you seemed to take it a bit literary. Hyped up on fighting talk. No good that, was it Major?

Quite so, VP.

Frustrating teachers is one thing, but this Summer Skool is not here to convert you to a life of delinquency. Waste a bit of time here, a bit of time there, just to make their already difficult tasks even harder. But no bullying, no violence. EVER. Not to teachers. And certainly not to other boys, your allies in the Mission; if you have to resort to such tactics you're missing the point. Those of you yesterday who were planning major disruption need to get this right, all we ask is a bit of quiet, subtle distraction. Small, understated actions. Nothing physical. Nothing illegal. Nothing that can't be misconstrued as boyish behaviour. This doesn't of course preclude playful pushing and shoving, which we shall use as a tactic in itself. Isn't that so, Major?

That's so, VP. Discipline is what it's all about, men. In any operation against more powerful opponents. Discipline. Clear objectives. And having principles.

So gentlemen, the Major and I are going to take you through The Magnificent Seven Principles you need to keep in mind whenever you undertake Mission tactics. OK, notebooks at the ready. Pay close attention. The first Mission principle in any task against an opposing force is no tough stuff. Quite the opposite. Always appear to be polite and reasonable.

There's a very good reason to appear to be reasonably good most of the time, gentlemen, especially when interrupting. Remember use a teacher's title "Sir" or "Miss". It makes you seem condescending to them even if we know you aren't. If things are slowing down, they are unlikely to sanction you if they think that you think that what you are doing or saying is reasonable. I'll just repeat that – it's NOT what teachers think is reasonable; it's what they think YOU think is reasonable.

It's NOT what a teacher thinks is reasonable; it's what the teacher thinks YOU think is reasonable.

Underneath it all, teachers are considerate types and are looking out for your mistakes so that they can help you to correct them. More about this in a minute or two when we talk about misconceptions. Anything to add, there, Major?

Only, VP, when on operations **Keep It Simple!** Simply; just keep it simple, men. At first, use only everyday things, like the pen (far mightier than a sword) and the books. No stink bombs and firecrackers, well not at the start. End of summer term, maybe, when all the teachers are demob-happy.

Thank you, Major. Our second principle covers ***misconception***. The universities teach teachers that pupils may not understand things straight away. Pupils learn by trying and making mistakes. Teachers are looking out for your mistakes and misconceptions. So don't disappoint them. Want to break up the flow of the lesson? Act dumb and come up with a question. The teacher might actually think you need help. You know what you are doing, the rest of the class know what you are doing, but the teacher doesn't. The only misconception is that of the teacher, who is unwittingly assisting with your tactics. Make the most of misconceptions – it's so powerful a Mission concept, it's almost poetic!

Better still, if a senior colleague is observing the lesson and sees you struggling, the observer won't blame you, they'll blame the teacher for not explaining it properly, and if things start to kick off they'll blame the teacher for lack of control. The more the teacher seeks to overcome misconceptions and fails, the less respect he gets from the observer. More pressure.

Our third principle is to misdirect the opposition. Can you pass me those over there, Major? What's this the Major has given me here? Watch very closely. How many gold coins do I have in my left hand? Correct, four. If I throw them into the air like this. Wait, I haven't done it yet. See they are still in my hand. If I throw them into the air, think about it, how many will land heads? How many tails? Half? Perhaps. Maybe not. WATCH! One, two, three… there now, up they go. Look! Still going up. Still going, going…

Sir, you didn't throw them.

OK, look. Nothing in my left hand. Nothing in my right. They can only still be going up…

PAUSE.

Where are they? Still NOT coming down. I've already told you. See, nothing in my palms. OK, I'll turn my hands over. Nothing at the back. The coins have left my hand and must still be going up… into space.

Rubbish! I mean that's not right, Sir. They'd hit the roof… S-s-sir. And bounce back.

Ah, but magic coins could pass through the roof, huh ceiling, couldn't they, gentlemen? By now they could be heading for *The Final Frontier*.

He's havin' a bubble.

You, yes you, front row. Look. Look carefully. Anything in my left hand? Anything in my right? Again see the backs as well as the palms. Those coins are not here. They are still heading up. You must agree? Tell them. Tell them, the rest of the class, what can you see in my hand? Nothing.

Nuffin'.

See – he's right. They're still going up. Now you, take this tin can and this stopwatch and come and stand over here. I'll start the stopwatch and put it in your right hand. Now hold the tin in your left. Arms stretched out. Just move over there a bit. That'll be where they come down in exactly 30 seconds.

Are you looking up for them? Check the watch? Look up. Watch.

CLINK, CLINK, CLINK.

Good catch! Your eyes must have followed them closely. Catching – you're good! Do you play cricket? Did you see them drop into the tin? Exactly on 30 seconds. Look in the tin. How many? Only three. Must be another somewhere up there! Taking its time to come down.

But, Sir, I didn't…

Round of applause for our volunteer. Sign him up as wicketkeeper! Well, done. Off you go, back to your seat.

But…

There you have it, gentlemen, four magic coins that can float up to space, a brilliant bit of catching… and this plain, ordinary tin can.

CLINK.

That makes four. They're all back. Thank you, gentlemen. Round of applause for our volunteer.

SLIGHTLY BEMUSED, MUTED APPLAUSE.

Now, I don't really think all of you believed me when I said that I could throw the coins miles into space. But they left my hands. Our volunteer held the tin. I was nowhere near. He caught them one by one in the tin. You heard them fall, one by one. So, if there's really no such thing as magic, floating coins, and I'm not powerful enough to launch them into space... through a solid roof. Then how was it done? Ponder that.

But I'll tell you something. What you have witnessed, gentlemen, is the classic magician's tactic of misdirection. You are busy thinking heads or tails, when that didn't matter. You are looking up, while something is happening at stage level. You are waiting to see something. But you hear something. The volunteer is watching the stopwatch, or looking up, or both. He isn't watching the tin. Nor my hands. Misdirection. It's a powerful tactic. Both for magicians, and for Mission Musketeers. While you do something, you make it look like someone else needs the teacher's attention. We'll bring misdirection in when we discuss Combo classroom tactics – it's a skill most boys seem to develop very easily. Now the Major General will take you through the more operational principles. Over to the Major... Major?

Huh, thank you, VP. Still can't see a hole in the ceiling.

Look to your troops, Major.

OK. ATTENSHUN. NOW! Stand firm, men. Eyes on the task in hand. Huh, operational principles. Misdirection, yes. Then there are... huh, pincer movements, undercover operations; yes, and having clear objectives and a fall-back position.

Pincer movements, men, require two or three distractions all at the same time. From different directions. Teachers just don't believe that boys can work so well together. Creates doubt and confusion. Nothing less.

For undercover ops, best look out for opportunities where

your tactics are unlikely to be reported. Men, keep yourselves under the school's radar. When a teacher doesn't know your name; if he confuses you with someone else, then your name is unlikely to go into the black book. Someone else's may, but hey!

Fix your targets carefully with a precise range and bearing. Carefully pick your time. Should you prosecute the Mission in every lesson? No, men, this can backfire. What if several teachers contact your parents to say you are causing trouble, all on the same day? An individual Mission Musketeer should stagger his tactics. After all there are 30 pupils in a class. No need to do everything yourself. Steady yourselves. Draw back and observe. Take a lesson out of the teachers' manual; differentiate. The VP will tell you what this means.

Yes, Major, differentiation, gentlemen. Teachers are advised to plan lessons with different exercises for certain pupils. But it's much easier for boys to differentiate, as in each lesson you've only one teacher whereas a teacher has 30 boys, all with different needs. Easy for us. Almost impossible for your teacher. Target one teacher this month, and then add a second next month. Creates self-doubt in the first, and lulls the second into a false sense of security. Major…

Final principle, men. No operation should be started without a fall-back position. Effective forces prepare for adverse outcomes. Don't ever become a mithering mugwort. Quickly sow some seeds. A week or two after you've started, tell your parents that Mr Godfrey isn't cutting mustard. You aren't learning anything with him. Big din in his lessons. It's the big lads at the back that won't fall into line. Only need to mention he can't control things once or twice, then let the idea simmer. Parents of Year 7s at a new school are particularly keen; ALWAYS asking what you've learnt that day – every day. When this topic comes up, then it's time to advance.

YOU will be taking a full part in old Godfrey's downfall, but your mother won't even consider that you're to blame. It's Mr Godfrey's fault for not having control. If she asks who are the noisy ones disrupting the lessons, then just tell her you don't really want to say. She'll understand. She doesn't want you to be bullied as a snidge by the big boys at the back.

The Magnificent Seven Mission Principles: Seem Reasonable – Have Clear Objectives – Use Misconception – Misdirect – Deploy Pincer Movements – Differentiate – Plan a Fall-back Position.

Take heed, men. A full out attack wouldn't ever work. Totally pointless. Only happens in St Trinians's films. The opposition is already occupying our territory, our classrooms. We are already surrounded; trapped within an unreasonable education system. Instead, active resistance should be our motto. Have clear objectives. Look for the weak points. Where, when, who? Then all push in the same direction.

And here's one last idea to leave you with. The Trojan Horse. You could make it look to teachers like you were friends bearing gifts, so they wouldn't expect you were up to anything at all. Ponder that.

It's the education system that's your enemy, and its foot soldiers, yes, YOUR teachers. That's my message for this morning, troops, nothing less. And when are teachers most vulnerable?

When they are having tea?

LAUGHTER.

Blithering bogweed, never the Staffroom. There you have teachers in numbers. I'll tell you when teachers are most vulnerable. When they are alone in the classroom, with the doors closed, that's when. And you outnumber them 30 to one, looking as though you're cooperating; yet really undermining the lesson.

OK. Time for a break. Sit up everyone. Stand. At the ready, front row advance in an orderly manner. Left, right, left, right... Next row. Off we go.

MARCHING STEPS.

Not sure the men really got that, VP.

They're boys, Major General, just boys. They were engaged, weren't they?

Quiet music can be heard in the background as the Major General steps aside. Fairly indistinct, but could be an unusual arrangement of Abba's Super Trooper.

A Lesson in Differentiation.

Settle down now please, gentlemen. Well the Major General's strategies certainly give us a lot to think about. It's great that we can have such a tactician with us at Summer Skool. Isn't he the very model of a modern major general? Cuthbert-Butterworth, related to the Duckworth-Butterworths, you know. Perhaps he'll join us again later in the week. Any questions, now?

Sir, why does the Major General keep talking about bogweed?

THANK YOU… let's keep on task. The Major General mentioned looking for the best openings, so you'll need to recognise teachers that are Mission targets and teachers that you don't annoy under any circumstances. Take careful note, now. As the Major advised, you'll need to differentiate.

People to be Extra Nice to.

Tell me, gentlemen, which teachers should you be nice to, always? Yes, you by the door.

The Head, Sir.

Of course. The Head. And the Deputy Head and the Assistant Head and the Assistant Head's Assistant and the Heads of Departments and… the rest of the Senior Staff. And why are they so very important? They help the Mission, that's why. Always be nice to them. They call themselves the Senior Leadership Team, SLTs to us. More about them again on Friday. Always make Heads and Assistant Heads feel that they are in control. If they ever take your lesson, you'll need to pretend to be model pupils; gives them complete confidence that the school's behaviour management system is watertight. Then, if a teacher complains about your behaviour, the Head may doubt the teacher not you. Think about it. A teacher with pressure from below – from you – and also from above; now that is a pincer movement.

As well as the senior staff, there are other adults to be extra nice to. If you see someone you don't recognise, then best to be extremely polite and helpful. These people could be anyone – school governors, local authority officers, Ofsted, the Head's third wife, anyone. Of course they may just be the local glaziers; come to fix another broken window.

Whoever they are, all are unsuspecting allies in the Mission. Give them a good impression at all times. If they think the pupils are polite, then they will question the judgement of any teacher that complains that school behaviour isn't what it should be.

They may even have come in for a one-off lesson to give you some interesting talk; a lot better than double-German. Such visitors include local celebrities, sportspeople, Zoe Ball's dad; oh and astronauts or scientists that make a bang. Or the army (also good at bangs) who get you dancing around to bouncy music, clapping in time and jumping about the hall. They can be really cool.

RUTs/RETs/RITs.

Other than heads, the full-time teachers at your school to be nice to include the RUTs, Really Useful Teachers, RETs, Really

Effective Teachers, and RITs, Really Interesting Teachers (also called Engagers). You may even prefer to please some, like Art and Drama teachers 'cause despite what I said yesterday their subjects can be fun, and they usually work in bigger rooms so you get to walk around and talk to friends. Also, if you want to be in the football team, PE teachers can be RUTs.

RETs have developed ways to counteract our Mission tactics. We don't think that they have any inkling of what we are up to, but one way or another they have built up these skills, most likely from experiencing and unconsciously analysing distracting behaviour. Some say it comes from within; it's something the Mission could do without.

RITs, Really Interesting Teachers, sometimes called ENGAGERS, are worth encouraging. If you have an Engager or a favourite subject, then there's no point in disrupting that lesson. Having some teachers that get you involved and hardworking can only help the Mission as it sets up self-doubt among the rest.

Awesomes & Enforcers.

Some teachers are held in utter, utter awe. Not by the pupils, but by the other teachers. Well at least the less-experienced, other teachers. Again PE teachers often fall into the *Awesome* category, particularly if they are still active in semi-professional sport.

If a classroom teacher is facing too much disruption, then in some schools he can ring for an Enforcer to remove the offending boy and take him to isolation. You'll just have to go along with these guys as they can be quite big. But you've done your bit, as removing you will certainly take time. Many schools used to give the Enforcer job to Deputy Heads, but there was too much waiting around. Some schools use ex-policemen or prison officers. But most just use an ugly PE teacher who's spent a bit too long in the scrum.

Funny how so many of these teachers not to be messed with – Awesomes, RUTs and ENFORCERS – spend a lot of their time in gyms.

Prime Mission Targets.

So now you know who NOT to cross, let's look at some of the teachers that make good Mission targets – the school wets. You'll understand why I say *wets* when I give you their nicknames.

Newts

NEW Teachers (NEWTs) include Student Teachers and something called NQTs. You'll recognise the first because they have proper lesson plans, there's always another teacher in the room, and they will introduce fairly interesting topics. They're very keen and, unlike Mr Godfrey, get lots of free periods to prepare things.

NQTs are newly qualified which means they have passed a few exams. They have the theory; unlike most of the older teachers you'll meet who have forgotten all the theory. During your lessons NQTs will try to demonstrate that they are meeting standards. Both Students and NQTs have standards. About a hundred, which the education authorities insist that they meet before they get properly paid.

Students and NQTs – not a lot of experience, but they certainly have their Standards.

There are potentially some very good teachers among the NEWTs. So you need to strike fast. Most have little experience of our tactics and aren't expecting them. If you can introduce self-doubt early in their careers, then they'll probably give up teaching altogether.

As newcomers, they really want to be wanted: by the Head, their colleagues, and – yes – you pupils. Some even feel that if they are friendly they will win you over; after all they can see more experienced teachers chatting and smiling to pupils and believe that's the norm. They don't realise that for boys to respect them, they have to earn it.

For pupils to respect teachers, teachers have to earn it.

Treat NEWTs as upstart newcomers, 10 minutes in the school compared to your years of service. They don't know all the ropes yet; but you do. Not only the ropes, but how to twist them.

Oldies

If you come across an old teacher, even older than your dad, who's NOT part of the senior team, then you can bet this teacher is either someone stuck in the same teacher's grade for decades or someone who's turned to teaching after an earlier job like rocket science, but found that that career just wasn't taking off. So they turned to teaching, full of confidence and misconceived ideas, not yet aware that boys can't be bothered with their subjects. With a little encouragement they could leave teaching just as quickly as they came into the profession.

Then there are ultra-experienced teachers who can't wait to give up and retire: they're the TOADS (Teachers on a Downward Slope), who need to stick with it until their pension is due. How can you spot them? New computer software. They can't be bothered. New behaviour systems. They can't be bothered. But don't mistake them for Toadies – you get them in every profession.

There's one other type of older classroom teacher. The Billy Goat Gruff. She's a good teacher, but can sometimes appear a bit gruff. Why isn't she a school leader? Perhaps, the Head has found her to be a bit of a nuisance; perhaps she asks too many questions during staff meetings or she actually reads the Union posters. Or maybe it's a male teacher who used to be a head of a department and your school Head and governors have decided to demote him to make way for new blood (that is someone cheaper). Either way, even though he's an excellent teacher, he's someone the school might like to shift. Mission tactics will be like pushing against an open door. Any complaints about the poor behaviour of boys from a GRUFF to the Head will be filed and forgotten. In fact the Head might secretly thank you for your efforts.

Supply Teachers.

Some days you'll have teachers who aren't your teachers. You'll recognise them because you won't recognise them. These are the Supply Guys. Do what you like in their lessons. Anything more than five minutes of learning with a Supply should sound warning bells to Mission Musketeers; you're definitely missing a trick or two. Supplies don't know your names, they don't know where anything is, they don't know where you sit. They don't know specific school rules. Simply by saying "but Miss Barnes lets us do that" will soon put them in their place.

Most are here today, gone tomorrow. You can have fun asking them for things like rulers, pencils, exercise books. They just won't know where your teacher keeps them. "In the cupboard in the corridor" is a good tactic. Either they'll leave the room in a confused state looking for cupboards or you can offer to help and go for a wander down the corridor.

When a Supply is in your classroom, school systems set up to protect the ordinary teachers will go out the window. Which is where some of you might like to try going for a laugh (so long as you're on the ground floor of course). Heads rarely acknowledge Supplies. Most full-time teachers are too busy to talk to them. Some schools just give them a slip of paper with things like "Period 3, Class 8XYZ, French". The Supply might be a Biology teacher. Je ne sais quoi, what?

Unlikely to make a fuss, hand out detentions or phone your parents, they're harmless; their main role is to give you a chance to practise the more extreme Mission tactics with little danger of any comeback. Use your time well in their lessons, gentlemen, to catch up with gossip, to practise games on your mobiles or to experiment with the optimum trajectory for a paper plane. You can even have a bit of sport by rushing around the room to get them in a spin. But always check when you don't recognise a new teacher, just to be sure. Satisfy yourselves that they are not *that* new teacher, about to join the school full-time next term. So at the start always ask "You supply, Sir?" Most will say "Yes" then quickly realise they shouldn't have done.

Mid-Termers.

Mid-termers are teachers that suddenly appear half-way through the year. Easy meat. They are often drafted in to take the classes of another teacher who's had enough. Or to free up an Assistant Head so that she can redraft the curriculum for next year to include Astrophysics (that Brian Cox has much to answer for). Not only will the mid-termers get difficult classes (that's why an Assistant Head previously took them) but everything around the school will be unfamiliar to them. They won't know your names, where you sit, which classrooms you should be in. It'll all take time for them to learn. Often they'll take your lesson this week in a different room to last. For the first few weeks at least you'll run rings around them. You'll probably find that they appear this mid-term, and just as quickly disappear the next.

Cover Teachers

Some schools now use full-time Cover Teachers to do the same fill-in jobs as Supplies, but they are permanently employed at the school, so they know your school's rules, have access to your behaviour reports and will be aware of the real troublemakers in your class. But the school will expect them to be all-rounders, to teach any topic, not just their speciality. So you can have fun catching them out. Why? Because often you'll know more about the subject than they do, like African Geography, where countries change their names every five years; and Physics, which most teachers never understood anyway.

This demonstrates one of our key points. Most teachers, when teaching an unfamiliar topic, are probably a bit rusty, which tells you that most of the academic stuff people learn at school they forget by the time they come to teach. So why should boys learn it in first place.

The good news is that as Cover Teachers belong to the school, you'll recognise them. The bad news is that they might recognise you. So don't be too disruptive; but be wary and have fun asking questions they can't answer.

So there you have it. Pick your targets carefully and you'll make a very valuable Mission Musketeer. Nice hot lunch, now. It's been a busy morning. You've all worked well. Lunch today is another special – mammoth fish bricks in double batter, chunky chips and lashings of ketchup. Yummy. Oh, and the fizzy drinks machine is taking 20p coins again. Back row can go first this time. Everyone stand. Out you all go. Those by the window first. Don't run. There are plenty of chips.

CLANKING OF DESKS. FOOTSTEPS. MUSIC.

Footsteps seem to fall naturally in line with the beat of the background music 'Revolting Children', from Matilda the musical.

CONCERNED LOW VOICE.
Restless bunch, VP.

> They are good and keen though, Godfrey, taking lots of notes.
> Perhaps just a few too many, VP.
> Stop fretting, Godfrey.

Always Play by the Rules.

GURGLING CHATTER. THEN... SILENCE.

Good to see you all looking…

> *You're new.*
> *Where did he come from?*

Yes, I'm new. But that's no excuse for your interruptions. Is it? IS IT!

HUSH IN ROOM.

Thank you. Let me introduce myself. I'm the Assistant Deputy Vice Principal at Summer Skool – here to take you through more of the classic tactics that you can use in your Mission.

First, let's see what you're made of. I'd like you all to stand up and waive your arms around in a figure eight. Up, everyone! UP NOW!

> *MUCH SHUFFLING. A FEW QUESTIONING COMMENTS.*
> *TWO MINUTES OF SWISHING AND SWIRLING, ODD WHOOP*

That's better. Get you geed up! Are you ready to rock and roll?

> *Yes, Sir! [IN CHORUS]*

Good. Right, good, here are some right rippers to slow down the start of a lesson. Specifically designed…

Hands down, boy. Urgh? You feel…?

Gloop! Gloop! I feel…
He's a pig, Sir. He had three fish bricks.

Quite. Yesterday the Vice Principal introduced you to the pen and book wheezes. Now, who can tell me what we call these slow start tactics, anyone?

RETCHING NOISE.

He's puking, Sir. All over the desk.

Couldn't you be sick during break? OK, take him out, someone. You, the boy in bright green…

MORE RETCHING.

Just bring him back when the choking has gone. We call these tactics… OUTSIDE NOW, please! And stop dribbling.

SCUTTLING FOOTSTEPS OUT OF ROOM.

OK, ready? We call them *SloPros*. Why? Because they slow down proceedings. Stop a lesson getting started. You… can we begin, please? Ready to rumble? Start taking those notes.

RESIGNED MURMURING.

Cheer up. Some sizzlingly good tactics to come. Rules. Everyone likes them. Don't we, boys? No? You should. If there's one thing we would encourage boys to learn as soon as possible, it's the school rules and standard procedures. Heads think they've been put in place to put you down. In reality they've been set up to make your class teacher's life a bit more difficult. Ponder this. Do minor school rules really matter? Of course they do. To the teacher. But as far as WE are concerned, maybe not. Infringing minor school rules will rarely get you anything more than a mild rebuke. But they can cut minutes out of a lesson. Pens at the ready. Good to go? Let's go.

Tactic Six – Dress sense.

Schools are always telling you what to wear; must have an odd sense of what's in fashion. They insist on the right coat, the right scarf, the right trousers, the right shoes, the school tie, or for the girls the right skirt (a right prime cause of conflict) and so on. They call it *dress sense*, we call it nonsense. It's traditional, and one of the first things teachers are taught in behaviour management is to be strict on uniforms: "pull them up on the little things like a sloppy tie and they'll think twice before trying on any worse behaviour".

Take advantage of the situation. Come in with the wrong tie, the wrong coloured shirt, the wrong type of shoes and you'll have your teacher discussing proper dress code instead of starting the lesson. Here your responses to "why haven't you got your school xyz on?" are particularly important. Have a snortingly-good excuse, something to do with falling over or what the cat has done or lending it to your brother or staying somewhere other than at home last night. These can take minutes off the start. But as the teacher's asked you, you can hardly be sanctioned for giving a lengthy, blow-by-blow answer. Just have the tie or whatever in your bag ready to produce at the appropriate moment. Rather than fill in extra time-consuming reports, if you eventually meet the dress code, teachers'll be reluctant to take it further.

Hey, we live in a cold climate, use that fact. Throughout the lesson try to get away with wearing extras like a football scarf; or wear gloves, especially the type with the fingers missing.

TACTIC SEVEN – REGISTRATION, AN OWN GOAL EVERY TIME.

SLIGHT PAUSE.

I can see you all jotting down these cracking tips. Good for more? Most schools will register you at the start of the morning and after lunch. Some each lesson, even. It's in the school rules. Stops boys from bunking off. So imagine the setting. Your teacher has got you all in through the door. She needs to get you engaged and to sort out the resources for the next part of the lesson. Also to log you in. A NEWT will understandably want to register everyone at the start of the lesson. More experienced teachers choose their moment. If they ever get a moment. Some schools demand that registration be completed within the first ten minutes especially for the first lessons morning and afternoon.

Now here's the problem. Many classrooms have only one computer which links both to the interactive whiteboard and the registration software. Ideally your teacher would like to start with the learning objectives on the board for the class to copy. Gets you settled. Instead up come everyone's names. Here you can make comments about some of the more obscure names parents give your classmates. However, even if you don't interrupt, school registration procedures are actually delaying the start, breaking up the teacher's flow. They are helping the Mission. It's a home goal.

Often during registration a teacher will ask a few pupils to call out their names. Maybe she can't put a face to a name, or she confuses a boy with someone with similar hair. If you have one of these *anonymous faces*, this should give you early confidence.

After she's registered everyone and is now back to the lesson, just as she's turning to what's displayed on the screen, it's your turn. Now you strike. "Miss, you didn't call my name." Even if she did, she'll stop to think and then waive you away. Someone else should now come in with a *Combo*, saying something like "He's right, Miss, you didn't mention him."

Note the use of the word "him". Never repeat the boy's name. Keep the teacher guessing. The teacher now has the dilemma. Should she spend another two minutes switching to the registration software again to check? She can't afford to miss your name off the register? Couldn't she jot your name down for later? No, the office needs registration right now.

If she's a NEWT she may not know your name yet. If she doesn't recognise you she can't register your name without asking. It's another distraction; another two minutes out of the lesson.

After the first term in Year 7, some teachers will know your names and log you all in without asking you to respond. A basic registration tactic here is for one or two of you to duck down below the desk. Pretend you're looking for something. Or just hide behind the big guy in front. Most teachers do a count-up. If class numbers don't match those on the computer, even an experienced teacher will need to check for boys she didn't see the first time.

You can also point out that someone is away. When the teacher says "No, he's not, he's in the corner", you can say "hadn't noticed him there; I was too busy writing down the learning objectives." The impression is that you are trying to be helpful, ready to work, whereas in fact you're creating an unnecessary delaying conversation.

Finally, try pushing it a little bit. A bit of chatter during registration is rarely punished, yet it will cause the teacher to look up and perhaps lose their place on the list of names. Few more seconds gone.

Tactic Eight – Name games, a good way to catch a NEWT.

Now here's another right zinger of a name game? Parents expect most new teachers, after one or two lessons, to magically recognise you, appreciate your talents and know the medals you won at Primary Sports Day. But new teachers teach up to 200 new faces. Those parents' evenings in early October can be a scream, particularly when boys don't go along – so many teachers have long discussions with parents not realising that they are talking about quite different boys.

Of course, teachers try to learn your names as soon as possible, certainly by the end of their first term. There are ways around this; on day one with a NEWT, just go and sit anywhere. He'll probably allow it for the first couple of lessons, just changing the class around to place some of the naughtier boys at the front. Teachers pay special attention to the names of anyone who is a bit noisy. So stay stum for a week or two and you'll fade into the background. Once your anonymity starts to become permanent, your teacher will be forced to adopt a number of *name tactics* suggested during teacher training.

The first teacher ploy for learning names is the seating plan. He'll tell you where to sit, who to sit next to. Use this. If he sees you in the wrong place and has to sort out where you all sit every lesson, then it'll knock off a few minutes while you reshuffle. Alternatively, stand in the aisle muttering "he's in my seat, Sir. Can you ask him to move?" Even if your mate is in the correct seat, it'll still deflect the teacher's attention away from what he was trying to do.

After a couple of weeks you might expect your teacher to have you all sitting where HE wants, alphabetically arranged from A to Z. No. Not so. In fact teachers themselves start to mess up their own system. First, they'll have to accommodate nerds and boffins that naturally migrate to the front to ask for more work, then there are the naughty boys that are moved to the front, then the daydreamers and fidgets that just need to be at the front. Within a month, the alphabet goes out of the window. Rippin' good, what? So then teachers need a Plan B.

Early in your first term in year 7 the school will want to photograph you. Now the teacher will have a face to your name. Some teachers even cut out each photo and stick them on a seating plan. If you can be away on photo day, so much the better. But most boys won't have an excuse, particularly as parents are keen for you to have 100% attendance at least for the first month and, well, they like to see their little boy's picture. So on the day of the photos, change your hairstyle, borrow your mate's glasses, puff out your cheeks, anything, just to change your features a bit. It'll be worth it as most schools use these first-term photos for at least four years. Look ahead to when you are in Year 10 and some

NEWT is taking you; what chance will he have of recognising a rough diamond from an angelic Year 7 photo?

Any questions? Yes, over there.

Can we do another figure eight, Sir?

TACTIC NINE – CANS AND FOOD.

Another key rule that just helps the Mission is no food in class. Try this. Works well after a break. Come in eating cake or drinking cola so it looks like you were just finishing off a playground snack. The teacher will need to delay what she's doing to ask you to stop drinking and to put the can in the bin. Now you can get up slowly, move casually towards the bin still sipping and then stand by the bin gulping and spluttering while you pretend you have to finish it.

An environmentally-conscious teacher might even have a recycling bin for cans. Think of the opportunities that can lead to – not just when you want to get rid of drinks containers, but every time you want to show how responsible you are by leaving your desk to recycle your worksheets.

If it's gum, then take it from your mouth and try to toss it towards the bin. But miss. You'll either be told to come out to pick it up, or if the teacher didn't see where it landed she'll be scraping her sole for the rest of the day.

Tactic Ten – Essential equipment.

Can we do another figure 8, Sir?

Not now. Just listen. This next tactic is a real glooper. Most schools give parents a list of equipment that pupils MUST bring to school every day. But of course any reasonable teacher knows that it's unreasonable to expect every boy to bring in every piece of equipment every day. Forgetful lot you are. So if you've forgotten your calculator, your art brushes, your PE shorts – it all takes time to sort out.

Some teachers keep spare rulers, calculators and so on. Another own goal! This gives you the excuse to stroll out to the front of the class to pick up a ruler, just as he's beginning to introduce the lesson. It interrupts his flow and the concentration of those nerds on the front row. Equipment tactics are ALWAYS effective. Use them daily. No teacher can deny you the tools for the task.

Tactic Eleven – School bags.

Bags mean bags of opportunities. Everyone carries one, and as we said the smaller the boy, it seems the bigger the bag. Teachers can't ban them from the classrooms as they carry your books, but most schools will have a rule that bags should be taken off as soon as you come in and then put under the desk, away from the aisles where teachers like to trip. So, your turn now, can you think of three ways to use your bag to slow down a lesson?

Silence.

Come on, any ideas? Yes, you in the grey hoody.

I'd leave it in the aisle, so that he'd have to stop to tell me to pick it up.

OK. Another, please.

Be slow in taking it off and I could bump into the boy next to me while doing it, Sir.

Good. And what might that lead to?

Teacher telling me to be careful?

Great, that's what we call a first-rate Combo initiator. The boy next door could then make a distracting noise as if you've accidentally caught him, or he could playfully push you back, thereby extending your bag tactic for a few more valuable seconds. We'll cover these when we develop Combos, later. You, over on that side…

Sir, I'd put my bag under the desk, then sit kinda ready for the lesson, then as soon as it's started I'd, huh, start to fumble with my bag to get my pen out.

Razzle-dazzle! You make it look like you're obeying the rules to the letter, when in fact you are using them to cause a delay. Brilliant. Now you over there…

I'd leave my bag behind and have to ask him if I could get up to go for it.

Sir. Please get into the habit of saying "Sir".

The hoody didn't say "Sir", Sir.

That was my mistake for asking a hoody... OK that's a few ideas. How about leaving your bag on your back, using it as something soft to lean back on? When the teacher asks you to remove it say "bad back, Miss, I need a cushion". Of course she'll challenge this; she might even ask you for a doctor's note. Whatever, it can take another minute out of the lesson just discussing how her request might lead to you becoming all hunched.

TACTIC TWELVE – ARRIVE LATE WITH AN EXCUSE.

This one needs setting up at the end of the previous lesson and is especially good if the earlier lesson is with a RUT. Even better if it's someone senior or an AWESOME. As you leave the earlier lesson, look for opportunities to dawdle a while – to wash up after Art or Food Tech classes, to log off your computer after ICT, to discuss school matches at the end of a PE session. As you leave the lesson, speak to the teacher about something relevant. You may want to clarify a point he's made or what the homework entails. It need only take a minute or so. Now you have an excuse for being late in the next lesson. As they keep telling you, "don't rush". Three to four minutes late. By now the teacher should have everyone settled; he'll have started to explain the topic for the day. When in you come! You can even quicken your pace as you reach the door, just to make it look like you've sprinted to get there. Then say: "Sorry, Sir, Mr Awesome kept me chatting about something important."

Class distracted. Teacher's attention deflected from his opening of the lesson. Everyone wondering what was so important. Yet your teacher's hardly going to question you. Most teachers will say something like "Get in; get started". It's rarely been known for anyone ever to get a sanction for talking to an Awesome about anything – it must have been important. Result, another two minutes lost at the start.

It's even better if you can emphasise the importance of Mr Awesome's words of wisdom in a way that prompts the teacher to ask what it was all about. If the teacher doesn't ask you for more details then a mate can butt in with "What did Awesome have to say?" and "Oh, that involves me too, Sir. Can I go and see Mr Awesome, NOW?" Of course, a good teacher won't fall for this, but even in telling you "No!" he's distracted from what he was about to teach.

I can see you smiling at the back. Got it. A real snorter, eh? Even better if you can delay your entrance until after registration. Then it's *double-rollover* time. Lesson stopped once for your arrival, twice for your mate's interjection. Oh and a third time for his switching back to the registration software. Do they have *triple-rollovers*?

So there you are – seven more classic openers. But did you know that you can also slow down a lesson even before you've entered the room. Not possible, I hear you say. Any ideas how you might do that? No? Well, just by being extra good, being *EARLY* you can make the lesson start *LATE*. Surprised. Listen on.

We asked "can we do another figure 8?" Sir.

ENOUGH NOW! I want to finish this set of tactics for when you arrive at the classroom door. Just one or two more.

Awwh! Sir!

Argue ye not, boys. Patience. There's some real spiffing stuff coming up.

Tactic Thirteen – Arrive early, on your own.

Now, you'd think that being early to lessons might help the teacher. Better than walking in late and upsetting his flow just as he starts the lesson. Well it aint necessarily so. There are occasions when being early can actually slow things down. When we told you about Mr Godfrey's busy day, we explained that teachers really need two or three minutes between classes to sort out their papers, resources, lesson plans. Just by arriving before the start of the lesson and talking to teachers in a friendly way, you distract them from this vital task. So when the bell goes and the rest of the class arrive, the teacher isn't quite ready. You'll know if this has worked by the way he or she has to rustle through lots of papers. Now let's consider...

Sir, thought that was the last one for now.

Nearly finished, just a bit of group therapy to go.

Tactic Fourteen – Arrive early, as a group.

If you can block the classroom door at the start of the lesson, then it takes everyone longer to get in. Result – a slower start to the lesson.

After your break, as the teacher returns to the classroom, a dozen boys crowding around the classroom door can form an effective barrier. A classic SloPro. Yet the teacher gets the opposite impression. You look as though you are all keen to start; but in reality you are using a slow start tactic. This is best done, not in an obvious way, but by untidy queuing outside the room, playfully pushing and shoving a bit. If the door handle is on the left, have one or two pupils stand just to the left of the door, slightly blocking the keyhole, and nudging each other in turn into the path of the approaching key. Most teachers will be carrying lots of books and stuff. Even better when they have a cup of tea in hand. Sometimes you can cannon another boy into the teacher causing a bit of a spillage. That's worth extra points, yes? And the odd remark like "Aww Sir, you've wet me" stacks the points higher.

The longer you can hold the barrier, the better. But it must never seem planned nor obvious. You're all being so keen to attend Sir's marvellous lesson.

So now you should be ready with 14 cracking tactics that stem not from being bad, just a bit forgetful about your rulers, drinks and so on. And many have involved doing good things like arriving early, helping a teacher to register you and asking questions about the subject. You'd have to be very unlucky to get a sanction for any of these. Yet together they can take up a good 10 minutes at the start of most classes. Slow down the start of a lesson and you are half-way to success because the teacher is now in a catch-up position and can get very flustered as the planned lesson needs to be squeezed into a shorter period.

SloPros – all it takes is just a few school rules, and a few friendly questions. Now I'll hand you back to the Vice Principal for any questions you might have about today's topics... Vice Principal.

Thank you, ADVP. He'll be back tomorrow, gentlemen, with a lot more tactics. What are you covering tomorrow, ADVP?

Tomorrow we'll look at some mid-lesson tactics, Vice Principal, including some old favourites like the 'Snitch and Snatch'.

A Bumping Noise. Then Footsteps Towards back of Room.

Can we have the Major General back?

Not now. Short chatter-break, gentlemen, while I get the Plenary notes.

General Chattering.

Plenary.

So, let's summarise. Today, gentlemen, we've looked at the types of teachers you'll come across in class. And I hope that you are starting to think about differentiating and dealing with each type. We also considered the magnificent seven underlying principles when carrying out Mission tactics. What were they now? Anyone? Just a few. OK. Altogether – repeat after me. Out loud. Be reasonable...

Be Reasonable.

Use misconceptions…

Use misconceptions…

Differentiate…

Differentiate…

And then we had joint tactics… which we call Combos. Altogether, Go, Go Combo!

Go, Go Combo…

Yes. A fairly full day. Time for your questions. You… in the red shirt.

Sir, what's that hen doing on the window sill outside?

We keep chickens.

Why?

For the eggs. Let's have a proper question about school. Hands up, now.

You said that if we like a lesson, then we don't need to disrupt it, like. But what if I like Art and he doesn't like it and he disrupts something I want to be getting on with like?

Politeness. Call me Sir, please.

Sir… if he…him over there…if he disrupts a lesson I want to be getting on with, Sir? What then?

Good. I like your question. Well said. Here, you may need to compromise. In your school, each boy probably doesn't want to be targeting more than two or three teachers. Why? Because you'll want one or two of the other teachers on your side. After a few weeks, the class will just know – I can't explain, but you WILL – you'll just know which teachers most pupils have targeted. Compromise and go with the flow. Next question, please.

I hate Science, Sir, what if everyone else loves it and I'm the only one wantin' to do tactics?

Everyone gets bored with Science these days. So probably that's hypothetical. Everything's simulated, YouTube videos, chemical modelling and the like. It wasn't always so. They used to let Science teachers blow things up and boys could play with acids and make smelly solutions; but all that went out when the Education Authorities decided they couldn't trust you. Tosh. As if you'd deliberately hurt yourselves. Why won't they let boys experiment, these days? After all, it is science.

Sir, why does the ADVP keep saying "good to go", but won't let us go?
Sir, Sir. Why does the Major General keep talking about bogweed stuff?

The ADVP and Major General are very experienced, gentlemen. Please do not question their methods, and I thought I told you to stick to proper Mission questions. Let's keep it relevant. You, over there...

Sir, you mentioned yesterday that we all look like average pupils. My numeracy teacher told me that we can't all be average.

You're right. We did say that most of you seem to be regular, average guys, good Mates. Your numeracy teacher was telling the truth. You can't all be average. In fact, half of you here are BELOW average.

GASP.

But the other half will be above average. Averages are just a concept. When it comes to categorising you, averages can be a bit MEAN. Let's get on with the next question.

MURMURING.

OK, I can see most of you asking yourselves "am I one of the below average pupils?" You will be in some subjects, but above average in others. It's only a statistical concept and like most statistics is lies, all lies, put out by mathematicians mainly to confuse you. Next question, please.

You said just now that our numeracy teacher was telling the truth. Now you say it's all lies... Sir.

Semantics. Your teacher was telling the truth when she told you a statistical mistruth. Can we move on?

But…

Take his name, Godfrey.

I've a question, Sir, about PE teachers. You said that teachers have little spare time what with preparing and giving lessons all day without a break. So, Sir, how come you said Awesome PE teachers have the time to play semi-professional sport?

When it comes to putting teachers under more stress, forget PE teachers. Best time to target teachers is when they are deep in thought. PE teachers rarely reach that stage. All they do is throw balls around and blow whistles. For PE teachers, life's a game. They're basically unstressible. And as we discussed earlier, a lot of them are awesome. The Assistant Deputy Vice Principal seems to have something to add.

Your question's a very good one, but it's a bit theoretical, as most boys like PE and so we don't tend to target teachers in PE lessons. Anyway, we can still use PE as an excuse to arrive late at the next lesson, "just getting changed, Sir" and all that.

Sir, if we are nasty to our teachers won't they mark us down in our exams?

Good question. We are getting some good questions, today. But no need to worry here. Teachers can't affect the really important exams like GCSEs as these exams are externally marked. For important end-of-year school exams for setting in Maths and English that are internally marked, then a lot of schools use moderation. This means that while the exams are set internally and marked internally, at least two teachers will see your exam paper, including one who doesn't teach you and probably doesn't know you.

And this reminds me of another wheeze: after an internal exam you can ask your parents to contact the school to see if the school will let them see your paper to help you to correct your mistakes. In such cases teachers will always check your paper again to make sure their marking was spot on. If the teacher has knocked a few marks off for a moot point, then he'll probably add them back in to avoid any arguments. Double-whammy result – a little extra pressure on teacher from parents… and you gain a higher grade.

How did you do the coin trick, Sir?

By magic, what else? It's an illusion, knowing can only lead to disillusion. We don't want to do that, do we? Bit of misdirection, that's all. Next…

Sir, when teachers really get stuck, can't they get help from other teachers?

Good question. With very little time to spare, teachers hardly have time to say "good-day" to each other. New teachers, even those that have pressing problems, pretty soon get this message and try not to pester their colleagues.

Sir, do you think I'll be below average?

Not again. Don't bother yourself, boy. That's it for today. Just… get yourselves ready to go home! Thank you, everyone.

CLATTER.

Everyone ready. Back row, in single file, orderly, orderly. Oh, and as you leave the gate tonight, gentlemen, look around for parents. Just be careful out there! You too, Godfrey. See you tomorrow. Row on the right first.

As the boys shuffle out, Madness's Baggy Trousers plays in the background. What fun!

Concerned Low-Voice.
Still frowning, Godfrey? What's on your mind?

Not sure, VP. Even the Major has a bemused look And... WHY does he keep on talking about bogweed?

Guess, too much time in the trenches, Godfrey... too much time.

Just be careful...

Day Three

Sanctions, What Sanctions? The Snitch and Snatch. Mr Godfrey is Saved by The Bell

WEDNESDAY, LESSON 1
Sanctions, What Sanctions?

Good morning. Good MORNING, gentlemen. OK. Let's start. I see Godfrey over there consulting his attendance sheets. He's nodding. Looks like all bar one here today. Is that right, Godfrey?

OK, later today, gentlemen, I'll be discussing how teachers plan lessons, but before that I'd like to tell you about a change for Period 3 today. Just after break, instead of the usual stuff, we are going to see what you've learned so far and how well it's sinking in. It'll be a bit of fun. Mr Godfrey, Mrs Benyana, Mrs Shah and Mr Higginbotham will each take a different group and attempt a lesson on USING ADJECTIVES. And you will be allowed to try out any SloPro tactic we've discussed so far. For this we'll move over to the Mission Tactic Practice Suites. They are the grey buildings beyond the chicken sheds.

But that's for later. Who is he Godfrey, the one that hasn't turned up yet? Henderson?

Sir, Sir, Henderson's not coming any more. Says it's not relevant as he's going to an Independent School in September.

Independents. Distort the whole education system, they do, what with their good attitudes and discipline. What, Godfrey?

Perhaps he's right, Vice Principal. He wasn't meant to be here. And… he's certainly one of the ones the Major General had his eye on.

Yes, quite, gentlemen. OK, back to what we've come here to learn. Quiet please. Let's concentrate now. YOU, you there. Sit down. Please be quiet!

SHORT PAUSE.

OK are we ready? You, yes YOU, you in the centre, still standing up. Can't settle, eh?

Give me a chance, Mush. Just sitting down…

What?

Give us, time.

DON'T YOU EVER DISOBEY ME! EVER!! YOU! You're in real trouble, me lad. Come out to the front. This moment. NOW!

No way.

Arguing? Better see the Head then.

COLLECTIVE INTAKE OF BREATH.
HUSH IN ROOM (LASTS TWO MINUTES).

And relax! Gentlemen, what you have just observed is a boy distracting the class and answering back to his teacher. As a consequence he was threatened with a sanction. OK, I'll let you into the secret; we arranged that little episode earlier. Well done, Firth, you'll make a good actor someday. Now, Firth was being a bit stupid answering back. Whoever the teacher is, NEWT or Awesome, he's almost certain to be given a sanction for such obvious cheek, even if only to demonstrate to themselves that they have a sanctions policy in place. It's inevitable. So what can we do about that? In this lesson we'll be looking at the times when teachers are really reluctant to sanction, times you can let rip with your tactics, ways to get round sanctions should your teacher insist, and what to do if you get an after-school detention.

Let's look at this printed list of behaviour sanctions produced by an actual school. This school told its teachers that it would support them in managing pupils' behaviour. It printed the list in the school diaries for everyone to refer to – parents, boys, teachers. Seems like everyone knows the consequences for bad behaviour.

BEHAVIOUR MANAGEMENT – SANCTIONS.
- LEVEL 1 (10 to 20 min detention) Break-time detention. (10 min) or Lunchtime (20 min) with teacher
- LEVEL 2 (45 min detention) After-school with teacher
- LEVEL 3 (1 hour)After-school with Head of Department
- LEVEL 4 (1 hour) After-school detention with SLT
- LEVEL 5 (2 days) Isolation   LEVEL 6 (2, 3 then 5 days) Exclusion
- LEVEL 7 Managed move to another school. (Expulsion).

I'll go into this in a bit more detail. The first level covers short detentions with your teacher; the second a longer one which would entail you staying behind, gentlemen, after-school. Both involve the classroom teacher who will have to stay behind to police your detention; in other words your sanction makes the teacher's busy day even busier, and results in more stress.

But apart from this it looks an effective school plan. If the Level 2 doesn't calm you down, then the school leaders are supposed to take over. Then there are higher levels where you face isolation, exclusion or you're shipped off to another school, maybe miles away. Now this *Sanctions List* looks like the ordinary classroom teachers have everything going for them. Full support! In black and white! If you misbehave, the school will back your teacher to the hilt in managing you, ridding his classroom of any disturbance to allow a calm atmosphere for learning. All the cards are stacked in your teacher's favour. What's more, they've even got your parents to sign that agreement to say they can do this to you. We argue that such a policy would be against your human rights, absolutely outrageous – if it worked.

Don't worry, our Mission tactics are designed to prevent any isolations or expulsions. Silent assassins rarely get caught. Nor special agents and boffins. That leaves the nerds and teachers often give them the benefit of the doubt. As for you and your mates, what should you do if your teacher is having a bad day and he just lets rip with a sanction? There's a very good chance you'll get out of it. Why? Not only do many of our more advanced tactics involve a bit of misdirection, the teacher doesn't know which boy to sanction, but also there are lots of times when teachers just feel unable to give you a detention. In reality, there's little time in a term to reach Level 4 or 5.

Times Teachers are Reluctant to Sanction.

In Bad Weather.

Did you know that boys play up whenever it's windy, drizzly or there's a storm about? Of course it's not true. Why should a bit of weather affect how you behave? However, and here's the interesting bit, most teachers believe that it IS true. Some universities have actually researched it to find what they call a correlation between weather and pupil behaviour. So if teachers are expecting it, let's not disappoint them.

When the weather's bad, you have the perfect excuse to run around more, push and shove each other, jump on and off walls. Have pretend sword fights with sticks, rulers, umbrellas. You can even splash that geek in Year 8 and few teachers will respond.

Not so sure? Here's a way you can prove it. Whenever the weather is a bit iffy, stand outside the Staffroom, pretending to discuss homework with Mr J or Mrs K. You'll hear teachers as they enter the Staffroom saying such things as "what's got into them today?" and "this weather sends them crazy!"

If you are unlucky and are pulled up for misbehaving on such days, then just remind the teacher "it's the weather, Miss, it makes us jumpy". She'll probably nod and agree with you. Next time it's raining, observe the older boys. You'll see them messing about. Join in. Keep the myth alive.

When Another Teacher Is Involved.

Sometimes two or more teachers will give you a lunchtime detention on the same day. Or you may have arranged to see another teacher at lunchtime for extra help or to finish something off. Now you can play one teacher off against the other. The NEWT will probably defer to a more experienced colleague. We'll cover this in more detail under the Double Bubble tactic later in the course. In the meantime, when threatened with a detention at lunchtime, it's always worth mentioning that you might not be able to come because you have to see Mrs Awesome. Then quickly catch Mrs Awesome in the corridor and ask to see her for help at lunchtime.

During Special Weeks.

Teachers can hardly give you an after-school detention in weeks when there are Parents' Evenings, school concerts, school trips and the like. Just not practical; the teacher hasn't the time to keep you back for an hour, then rush off to the Hall to meet the parents.

Some weeks, teachers are busy writing reports after school. We could do a whole lesson on the art of writing reports, but all you need to know is that teachers' reports generally follow a watered-down, prescriptive format to avoid any prospect of libel. Anyway during report writing weeks, teachers are very busy after school and detentions just get in the way.

Then there is the first week of term, when teachers give pupils the benefit of the doubt while they settle in, and the last week of term, when they've run out of evenings to keep you in. And what about exam weeks? Surely you need your evenings for last minute revision – yeh, urgh!

So what can happen when you don't turn up? You might expect a no-show from a really bad boy or a silent assassin, but isn't it a bit risky for you and your mates? Well, not necessarily.

A non-attendance needn't look like sheer disobedience. Boys are forgetful, have a lot of other things on their mind and anyway you're not usually much trouble. If the teacher presses the point then use the "I forgot, Sir" excuse – with a smile. As we said, there's a very good chance you'll get out of it as the first two sanction levels involve the teacher in even more work. Not only will he have to give up another break, lunchtime or another hour after school, he will also need to write a behaviour report on the central computerised record system – always a bit of a palaver. This can take 10 minutes per pupil plus the 10 or 20 minutes while you serve your detention. What's the likelihood that he'll want to give up even more of his own time by giving out a lot of detentions? Particularly as he's already spent one lunchtime in vain waiting for you to turn up.

It's the same for the after-school detentions. Another wasted hour of a teacher's time. But can't the teacher sit there working while you serve your detention? Hardly, as if there's more than one boy in detention there's sure to be some distraction going on. OK, a tough teacher might stop the detention as soon as you make a sound and put you up to the next level. But that's very harsh and most teachers won't go there as they feel that they are being unfair.

As for the other levels on the list they rarely occur. The SLT don't really want to be bothered minding some other teacher's problem pupils. So the system is biased against any sanction level above those that involve the classroom teacher.

[Dear Reader: at this point the Vice Principal gives a very cogent argument to show that any School Sanctions policy with more than three levels will probably fall apart. A blow-by-blow, week-by-week account that took him a tedious 20 minutes to explain and received

several yawns from the boys. If you're really interested, if your school has a 3+ levels policy, then we've transcribed it in full in Appendix G. Back to the VP's speech...]

... in a nutshell, gentlemen, any boy that toughs it out and doesn't attend detentions will get away with it. After a term or two at a new school, ordinary classroom teachers such as Mr Godfrey realise that the detention system can't really work, so they become discouraged, doubt comes in "why doesn't the school behaviour system support me?" and they wise up and cut down on giving detentions. Any forward-thinking teachers will find any excuse not to give detentions as it costs them more time than the pupil.

PHONING HOME.

So what sanction can a teacher adopt to deter pupils from disturbing lessons? They can phone your parents to discuss your behaviour, that's what, gentlemen.

Atrocious, yes, but you can relax, even this is often ineffective, as teachers are told to use the school phone for such calls (stops you getting their mobile numbers). But, when the school is open, most parents are out at work or shopping or collecting your younger sister from playschool. 4.00pm is when teachers tend to make most of their calls. They take a deep breath, steady themselves and speak firmly and sternly... to an answering machine.

But some parents will be in and this can be a bit embarrassing. Only a bit, though. Teachers are taught to be positive when speaking to parents. They mustn't infer that you are totally bad. It's the behaviour that's bad, not the boy. Instead they need to make one or two nice comments before they drop you in it. As a result parents get a mixed message and never really understand how distracting you've been. Some come away thinking the teacher has phoned to praise you.

If speaking to your parents is a worry, you can always rush home early and answer the teacher's call yourself saying "I'll pass on your comments to my mother".

What with your teacher hanging around for pupils and having to make sanction reports, sanctions cost a teacher much more time than the pupil. Sanctions waste the teacher's time. They also create doubt in the teacher's mind over the school's sanctions policy. Sanctions were made for the Mission!

That's enough for now on sanctions. It's time to look at Lesson Planning. Something every teacher does, for EVERY lesson. At least when Ofsted are around. Short chatterbreak now, while I get the next PowerPoint up.

Aren't we having a break now, Sir?

Teachers have been known to plan lessons.

LESSON PLANNING AND THE MISSION TACTIC PRACTICE SUITE.

OK. I'm ready now. QUIET! NOW! No, the break comes later. Wait and see. BECAUSE when we've finished this lesson you won't be coming back to this room for Lesson 3. It'll be time for you to show us what you've learnt so far. Time to dip your toes into the water. Exciting, eh, gentlemen?

After break, you will make your way directly to the MTPS, Mission Tactic Practice Suites. Mr Godfrey and three other vict..., sorry volunteer teachers, will give you a Year 7 English lesson on ADJECTIVES and how to use them. We initially thought that a lesson on irony might be appropriate to Summer Skool, but adjectives seemed a bit easier. It's for a middle set so some of you will sail through it; some might learn a bit about English language. A bit – not too much, now – concentrate on the tactics, not the topic.

Mr Godfrey's group will be in Suite S1. We've tried to keep best mates together. The three lists telling you who goes where are on the wall at the back. Others will go to Suites S2 to S4. Each class of about 30 boys. No seating plan. During break, get together with your mates to plan your tactics.

OK, let's resume. What's this I'm holding here? Now here's something boys don't often see. Neither do a lot of teachers. Only joking. This bit of paper is called a *Lesson Plan*. On many a Staffroom wall, they hint at the value of lesson plans with slogans like "*Fail to plan, plan to fail*". It's a well-known fact that every teacher, every lesson, every day, will prepare a ***very detailed*** lesson plan to very precise Ofsted standards. How they do it no-one knows. What with preparing special resources for each group, it can take about two hours for each lesson and summarises what your teachers want you to achieve, how they split the topic up into smaller parts. And how they intend to differentiate between the different abilities of each of the 30 pupils. It's a common occurrence to see lots teachers working on these plans, all around the Staffroom, a plan for every lesson, beautifully annotated... in your dreams. *GULP.*

Here's Mr Godfrey's plan for this morning. It's a six-part lesson, each part will take around 10 minutes, possibly 12, but certainly no more. That's 'cause someone once worked out that YOUR attention span is likely to be just one minute more than your age. Where do they get these theories? Try telling an 11-year old boy to ease off after 12 minutes of Car Crashers 2016 or any other race and chase computer game.

I'll put Mr Godfrey's lesson plan on the board here. It starts with his title *UNDERSTANDING ADJECTIVES AND ADVERBS.* Then he lists the time and date, plus any children in the class that might need special assistance.

Below this he states his learning objectives; that's what he wants YOU to learn:

- I will be able to recognise the parts of speech we call adjectives and adverbs.
- I will understand the difference between them.

- I will be able to use them to make my sentences more interesting.

OK, look at the board now. The asterisks next to some times denote opportunities for the teacher to see if you've started to understand the topic. He'll try to do this sneakily without you even noticing. It's called Formative Assessment or Assessment for Learning and will tell him how successful he is in putting the topic across.

He's labelled his six parts A to F, each listed against his estimated time of delivery. The notes next to each item are for HIS guidance only; boys never knowingly see these lesson plans.

LESSON PLAN – *Adjectives and Adverbs*
Class S1 (AFL)*

ENTER

Class enters and settles.

1 min

A – Starter activity/Registration. Resource A (Level 4/5) *

11 min

START MAIN LESSON

Introduce concept of adjectives and contrast them with adverbs. When to use them to best effect. Ask class for ideas.*

16 min

B – Fill in the blanks (Resource B) (pairs)

25 min

C – Writing practice – essay

(Textbook, Exercise 14.3)* [Level 5/6]

40 min

D – Peer marking (pairs)

45 min

E – Whole class discuss work (and reward)*

50 min

F – PLENARY

55 min

Collect essays *. Dismiss class

Of course the times he's planned may change depending upon how the lesson goes, but you get the idea.

Now, let's look at the plan a bit more closely. For his starter, Mr Godfrey has produced a resource. That generally means a bit of paper for you to scribble on while he gets his head around what he hopes to do next. In this instance his resource is a *Wordsearch* worksheet full of, well, words. You have to circle the adjectives and underline the adverbs. He won't tell you the difference yet. He just wants to assess your prior knowledge (that's what the asterisk means). While you complete the *Wordsearch* he will use his computer to register your attendance. On 11 minutes is where he needs your quiet attention while he explains the difference between adjectives and adverbs. He plans to keep this very short as most boys prefer to get on with things rather than listen to teachers spouting the finer points of English language. He's also included time for questions and answers. Again watch out, he's secretly assessing your understanding.

After 16 minutes he intends to hand out another resource. This time it's a load of sentences with blanks in them. The first says "The … fox jumped over the … dog", the second "The … dog … chased the … cat around the …room." You have to work in pairs and put some words in the blanks. At the same time he expects you to discuss what you are doing quietly with the person sat next to you. In theory after seven or eight minutes he wants to collect them in; but he probably won't, so don't screw them up yet as this might reduce their aerodynamic properties.

Then he'll quickly ask you to write an essay of at least two sides using as many adjectives and adverbs as possible. The textbook Chapter 14.3 gives you several essay options, such as *'My journey to school'*, *'The best book I've ever read'* and *'Killer creatures from Upper Tooting'*. Only joking with that last one. At this point in the lesson you're on your own. Heads down and writing like madmen, or so Mr Godfrey hopes.

Around 40 minutes he wants you to swop your exercise books with your neighbour who will underline relevant adjectives and adverbs in your essay and discuss with you why you've used that word and the benefits it brings to the sentence. You will give your partner a point for every appropriate adjective and adverb and Mr Godfrey will ask you to tell him how many you've managed to use. Then there are three or four minutes for everyone to discuss the topic as a whole class. This you do by making comments or by asking questions, one at a time, with Mr Godfey coordinating what the other members of the class think about your answers.

Finally, after 55 minutes Mr Godfrey intends to recap the main points of the lesson in his Plenary. He will get you involved and may ask you to write down something you understand now that you didn't at the start of the lesson. I know how Mr Godfrey works. Sometimes he asks the class to write one or two sentences that you might say to the Head if he met you in the corridor just after the lesson and he asked about what you had done in English.

And at the end Mr Godfrey will collect your essays and dismiss you in an orderly fashion. So that's his lesson. Minute-by-minute. Lesson plans guide the teacher and prepare an observer for what to expect and when. It is your Mission to frustrate such planning. Any questions?

What's that mean?

That? It's probably a restrictive relative clause.

Huh? No, Sir. That! At 45 minutes it says "and reward". Do we get prizes?

I guess Mr Godfrey intends to reward the writer of the best essay and most likely knowing Godfrey it'll be with a Mars Bar. OK. Any more? No? Good. The MTPS is in the West Wing; turn right just beyond the refectory area, then head straight on at the chicken runs. Remember Mr Godfrey will start his lesson prompt at 11.30 am.

Don't be late, now. He'll use a number of behaviour techniques to get you engaged and on task. Look out for them and use the appropriate counter tactics. During Mr Godfrey's lesson, you'll see me sitting at the back. This is called an observation. Teachers love observations. But I won't be observing Godfrey this time. I'll be observing you and I will stop proceedings from time to time to comment on how effective you are being at slowing down the lesson and to give you any tips. Remember that while it's Mr Godfrey's learning objective to teach you to understand English, yours is to introduce the 3Ss. Good luck.

Time for a slightly longer break to allow you to prepare and walk over to the MTPS. Get some cola down you now. Check which class list you are on and see you all at 11.30.

The use of ADJECTIVES and ADVERBS.
A lesson given by Mr Godfrey

OK, Lads. Don't crowd the door. Why are you here so early? Don't you have anything better to do than stand around in corridors? Don't push, please. You – to the back. And you. Let me get to the door. Gawd, I've dropped, now I've…

Sir, you could have scalded him then with that tea.
Yeh, 'ealth and Safety.

Pick up my papers, please, laddie. Thank you. Do it now, not next week please. Yes, YOU!!

OK, suit yourself. Thank you, Sunil. Just pick up a few books and pop them on my desk. Please wait outside while I get things ready for the lesson. Just wait there! I asked only Sunil. Stop pushing him through the door. YOU, wait outside until you're told.

CLAP OF PAPERS DROPPED ONTO DESK.
CLICK. (COMPUTER TURNED ON)

What are you doing? I asked you to stay outside until I'm ready.

Please Sir, who do you think has stretched his gum the furthest? Look, Sir, at mine. Not his. This one. I'm first. Stop pushin'.

In the bin with that. OK, OK, just get inside. The rest of you can come in now. Not all at once. Quietly take your seats. Settle in. These are for you to… I have some… Stop running around, please. I've got these Wordsearch sheets. Jessie, can you distribute them to your row. Atill, these are for your row. Liam, take these.

NOW please, lads! We can't wait all day. Chop. Chop. Come on. Why are you so slow?

You asked us to not run around, Sir.

Well step to it now. Come on… OK, thank you Sunil, you hand them out. Top fellow. You may as well take them all.

Wordsearches – the last refuge of…

So boys, when you get your worksheets I want you to work quietly for 10 minutes and show me what you know about adjectives and adverbs. LIAM!! Sunil is doing it now, stop trying to prise them off him. OK, just a few, Liam.

Look it's five past already and some of you haven't even started.

We haven't got the sheets yet, Sir.

OK let's see who's here. Why won't this thing come on? OK. Josh Albright. Liam, hand out the books nicely. Don't throw them. Look you've just caught Nathan under the nose. Josh. Is Josh Albright here?

Yes, Sir.

Speak up, lad.
You asked us to be quiet.

Benson… Wesley Benson?
Here… Sir!

Yes, Nathan, you can go to the toilet to get some tissues to stop the bleeding. Who's next? Yussuf…
Sir, I've got no pen.

Here, Dev, take that.

WHIZZ.

Yussuf D. Are you here?

118

I'll just stop things there, Mr Godfrey.

Yes, Vice Principal.

Did you see what Mr Godfrey did then, gentlemen? Although he's concentrating on the register, he's pre-planned for boys without pens and has several on his desk ready to hand out. As he's busy though, he tossed it to Dev.

Dev, great that you used the *No Pen* tactic, but you missed a bit of a trick. Instead of catching it, you might have dropped it to cause a short pause or better still have fumbled it. I know you're in the cricket team, Dev. Just a bit of a fumble, so that it lands on Ben over there. Deliberately, I mean. Ben could then have come back with "Sir, what's he doing?" thus taking the teacher's attention away from registration. And if feeling optimistic, Ben might then have followed up with "Sir, Sir he hit me with a pen. What are you going to do about it?"

But so far, so good. Particularly liked the way you started early. And well done that boffin, with the gum trick. It's 11.44 now and Mr Godfrey is still taking names several minutes after he was supposed to start the main part of the lesson. Thank you, Mr Godfrey. Continue with the lesson.

Yussuf . Are you here? Good fellow. Thank you.

Chan?

Chan, err. OK I'll put these in without calling out names. Just get on quietly with the wordsearch. What's up, now?

Got no pen, Sir.

Here… Mika.

WHIZZ. FUMBLE.

119

Sir, he hit me!

Time's up. It's 11.50 now and we haven't finished our Starter. Better hand them in. Did you all get ten or more words? Anyone with 20?

Sir, I haven't got one.

Not a single word?

No, a wordsearch.

Thank goodness, thought for a minute you were asking for another pen.

Huh…huh…huh… [HALF-HEARTED LAUGHTER]

OK, lads. Exercise books ready. Open them and write today's date and the title that's up on the board. Then write the learning objectives. All three of the objectives. Liam can you go and collect in the wordsearches?

I haven't handed them all out yet, Sir.

Just sit down, Liam. I'll collect them later. Now, can anyone tell me what the difference is between an adverb and an adjective?

We're still writing the objectives, Sir.

Just get on with it. The difference. Anyone?

No-one? OK listen, please. Well, an adjective is a word we usually place before a noun to help to describe it. Instead of "The fox jumped over the dog" we could say "The quick, brown fox…"

What are you doing? Take your rucksack off his desk.

Just getting my planner, Sir, to write down the homework'.

I didn't mention homework. But as you've mentioned it you can all…

BOOO!

Quiet! Put that rucksack away. NOW! I was about to say "The quick brown fox jumped athletically over the lazy dog." This tells us a bit about the fox and how active he was compared to the dog that was sleepy or just plain lazy, lying in the sun.

You didn't mention sun, Sir.

Well he was more likely to be sleeping out in the sun than when it's pouring down. Am I really getting into an irrelevant conversation with you, lad? Let's carry on.

KNOCK.

An adverb gives us extra information about the verb. The fox didn't just jump over the dog… *KNOCK…* he jumped athletically. While you're still writing your notes, I'll put a pile of worksheets on each of the front desks. Pass them back please. Don't throw them. Don't snatch, Liam.

KNOCK!

Yes, come in!

Sorry I'm late, Sir.

Late? It's nearly tomorrow. [CHUCKLING – FROM GODFREY.]

HALF-HEARTED LAUGHTER FROM BOYS.

Sit down quick or it'll soon be next week. [GODFREY'S CHUCKLES TURN INTO GUFFAWING]

You're not supposed to laugh at your own jokes, Sir.

Sorry, lads, I always laugh at my own jokes as I… [MORE BUBBLING FROM GODFREY] make them up on the spare of the moment and… [UNCONTROLLED LAUGHTER] it's the first time I've heard them myself.

TWO MINUTES OF BURBLING, HUFFING AND INSINCERE BOYS' CHUCKLING, WHILE GODFREY RECOVERS HIS COMPOSURE.

Yes, OK now. What, lad?

Can I come in, Sir? Sorry I'm late.

In, quick, lad. No, I don't wish to know how your shoe split. Sit down here. Stout fellow. Now each of these worksheets has blanks for you to fill in with words to make each sentence more interesting.

Quickly, Sir?

Huh?

Should be "in quickly", Sir. It's one of them adverbs... or an adjective, Sir. You should never say "in quick".

Good... *[SIGH]* I'll continue. Your words on the worksheet will be adjectives or adverbs. If you like you can write the adverbs in blue and the adjectives in pencil. Look for words that you could use to describe nouns and verbs to make the sentence more interesting.

I haven't got a blue pen, Sir.

Try another colour. Any colour. Pass them back now. Please don't throw them. Why are you getting up?

He knocked them on the floor, Sir.

RESIGNED GASP.

Pick them up. Now, I can see some of you writing away at the front. The rest need to catch up. I'll give you five minutes.

Sir, is "blue" an adjective?

Does the word "blue" describe something? Yes. It does. Blue IS an adjective.

Shouldn't we be writing the adjectives in blue, then, Sir. It looks a bit funny writing "blue" in pencil and other words that aren't adjectives in blue.

Be a good fellow, do your best, boy. The colours are immaterial.

Thought you said that colours are adjectives and they were important.

What are you doing now? Get back! Sit down!

Getting a coloured pen from Plumb. He's lending me one.

I just need you all to write **AS MANY WORDS AS YOU CAN IN THE SPACES**. You've got two minutes left. Get on with it!

OK, pens down. Now let's discuss what we already know about adjectives and adverbs.

You just told us to pick up blue pens, Sir. Now you're telling us to put them down.

Swop your sheet with the boy next to you and together count how many words have been filled in. As you are doing so, discuss with each other why you think the word you've used is appropriate and whether it is used adjectively or otherwise.

CHATTERING.
FOUR MINUTES PASS. LOUDER CHATTERING.
DISTURBANCE. SOMEONE CALLING OUT.

Could I have your attention, please? COULD I HAVE YOUR ATTENTION? NOW! Thank you. Who came up with over 20 words? 30 words? Yes. 33? That's good. Please bring your sheet out and we'll discuss…

What are you doing? Not you. YOU. Over there! What are you standing up for, fiddling about like that?

Just fixing the blinds, Sir. The sun is bright.
Right in his eyes, Sir.

Can I interject again here, Mr Godfrey?
Vice Principal. Yes.
Well gentlemen, we hadn't covered the blinds and windows routine yet, yet that boy seemed to use it. Where did you get that from, boy?

Dunno, think it came naturally, Sir.

Name? Your name?

Justus, Sir.

Well, Justus, I'm impressed. Back to you, Mr Godfrey.
Thank you, Vice Principal. Where were we? What are you doing here, hovering around me, boy?

Marks… Sir. I have 33. You were checking.

No time for that now, boy. Go and sit down. Let me see. What's next? Ah, yes. Please turn to… urgh … urgh. Where's my textbook gone? What's it doing there?

I needed it, Sir.

You've already got one on your desk.

He's on another page, Sir.
Just trying to do my work. Can't do anything right here.

Give it back, now. Please turn to Exercise 14.3 on page 127. It gives you several suggestions for essays. You can choose any you like. Then write two pages of A4 with as many adjectives and adverbs as possible. 15 minutes. Quietly, pens poised, heads down, off you go.

YOU, come out. Change places with him. I need you to concentrate and that means THINKING quietly.

RELATIVE QUIET. FOUR MINUTES OF COUGHS AND SNUFFLES.

Sir, is this an advert?

Adverb. Stay there, I'll come and look … what the …?? Whose is this bag?

SNIGGERING.

Did you swear, Sir?

Who left that bag there?

I think you swore, Sir.

You and you. See me after. After-school detention for the both of you! Stay behind at 3.30.

Thank you, Mr Godfrey. Thank you, gentlemen. All very interesting. Saved by the bell there, Godfrey.

Stay. STAY! Whoa, gentlemen. That bell was just for the MTPS. Didn't mean you can go. Well done, gentlemen. You knocked a good 20 minutes off Godfrey's lesson, which is brilliant for a first try. How natural these things come to boys. We'll debrief first thing tomorrow, when I will have the reports back from the other observers on how you've all done.

And... AND... as you knocked 20 minutes off Godfrey's English lesson, I think you deserve an extra 20-minute break for lunch. Extra rumble crumble. No rushing, please. Orderly fashion. See you back in the usual classroom for Lesson 4 when the ADVP will take you through some mid-lesson tactics. I said, "No rushing!"

EXCITED CLATTER.

Footsteps fade into the distance to the sound of 'Let's get ready to rumble' a version of the classic by PJ and Duncan, (more commonly known as Ant and Dec – knew they'd get into this somehow).

A QUIET ASIDE
The Major is beginning to agree, VP. Said he could feel it in his guts.

If ever a man had guts, Godfrey, it's Cuthbert-Butterworth.

Combo tactics for once a lesson is underway.

Everyone good to go, this afternoon. Played blinders this morning, boys. MTPS was poppin'. VP said you'd knocked a cracking 22 minutes off... *[CHEERING]*, settle now, folks. I can see you're still all excited. And I see more of you have been down to the pens; can you please not get feathers all over the carpets?

Now if those early tactics got you excited, just wait for what we have next. It's time to Combo. I'll start when we settle a bit.

PAUSE FOR SILENCE.

Some teachers, some schools, have tactics to hit the lesson running. A strict start to a lesson in every sense. This can certainly upset any SloPros. So as not to get caught almost as soon as you've entered the room, you may need to play it safe for 10 minutes. Wait until the lesson is underway.

OK. You looking good to go. I want you to imagine your classroom. Thirty pupils. Heads down. Quietly working. Everyone's on task and writing furiously. By some means, the teacher has got you all engaged. Mission-wise this is a disaster! How can we break this up?

Should someone put his head above the parapet with a solo tactic? Brave move. Bit dicey, perhaps; risks being singled out for a heavy sanction. However, we can't let this total class engagement continue. All's not lost. It's just what Combos were designed for. Combos – the most powerful tactics devised to break up the flow of a lesson.

COMBOS.

Where should I start? When several boys get involved in a joint tactic, we call these Combos. They're brilliant. Why? Because if you use a tactic on your own, then the spotlight will fall on you. That may be what you want, but an alert teacher will know exactly where to direct his laser-like gaze. Now you are THE totally obvious, one-and-only candidate for a detention. Daft, that. But with Combos, several low-level distractions are going on at the same time. Teachers literally don't know where to direct their sanctions. Combos confuse! The lesson stalls. Self-doubt and Stress start to creep in. Three Mission objectives all at once! But the superoonee, main benefit of Combos is that they protect you from any major sanctions.

Let me explain. As I said, if a single pupil pipes up and interrupts the lesson, then he could become the focus of attention. However, Combos divert the teacher's attention away from the primary tactic and from the real perpetrator to the whole class. In effect, they disperse the teacher's annoyance and dilute any consequential sanction on an individual.

Anyone can start off a Combo; you can arrange before the lesson who will go first or just play it by ear. But once a mate starts a tactic, don't leave him on his own to face the music. He's signalling that he has a plan and now's the time for you to help.

You can do Combo tactics in twos and threes; half the class, even, if you're feeling confident. Remember, the more people that get involved, the less likely any one pupil will get sanctioned. That's because teachers are told not to give whole-class detentions as it's unfair on the nice quiet guys who are getting on with their tasks. A basic principle behind Combos is that the severity of the sanction on each individual boy is inversely proportional to the number of boys taking part in the disturbance.

The severity of a sanction is inversely proportional to the number of boys taking part in the disturbance.

Ready. First, a few delaying Combos to knock minutes off a lesson, then we'll look at how Combos deflect the blame away from you, including even ways to deflect the blame for your distractions onto the teacher himself. Finally, there will be days when you just can't stand it in your classroom any longer, so we'll look at tactics that can be used – against all school rules – to get you out of there. Good to go. Let's Combo.

TACTIC FIFTEEN – THE 'SNITCH AND SNATCH'.

This is one of our favourites. A real spiffo! Teachers never punish boys for over exuberance. Use this fact. Look keen when passing things around the class, like worksheets and books. Instead of passing things calmly between yourselves, try snatching, dropping, pushing and shoving. You look keen as though you're trying to get on with it, whereas in fact you are slowing things down. A useful Combo is the *Snitch and Snatch*. He snatches something from you, you then have an excuse to shout out to the teacher that you've been wronged and someone has taken something you needed. Point the finger at a mate; he won't mind you snitching. He'll just shake his head and look bemused. Or the two of you can start an argument.

"Sir, he took my pen lid."

"Sir, he took my ruler."

"No, I didn't. Sir, he's lying."

Try it. But get your mate's agreement first. Takes a minute or two for the argument to develop and for the teacher to sort out.

TACTIC SIXTEEN – HAVE A VOICE.

A totally quiet, attentive class is a teacher's dream. Dream on. Noise happens in every lesson. Some teaching theories even talk about the benefits of a noisy classroom where pupils are busy discussing the topic of the lesson, analysing problems together, debating outcomes. But that's planned noise. As soon as the teacher turns to look at the board you can take it as a signal to up the noise levels with chatterbreaks or some special noises. A chatterbreak. It's as simple as chatting to the boy next to you. You'll have lots to talk about anyway, like whether that Spurs' goal should have stood, or the next level of ThunderFighters V. And if you are near the front and don't want to be told off, just chat about the topic.

Soon the ambient background noise in the room will increase. It's called the *Cocktail Party Effect*. Two people talk quietly to each other, then another two, then more. As each pair chats the background noise increases, so they have to talk a bit louder to be heard over the increased levels. Soon there's quite a noise in the room.

The teacher now has to deal with this. And it all takes up time. Good, eh?

OK, now you can get involved with some special classroom noises. All good Mission Musketeers need to make their voices heard. However it's good to have one or two special voices. Have an *I must be stupid* voice, or a doubting voice, or a *really-Sir-can-that-be?* voice. This infers the teacher's missed something (good tactic for boffins to perfect). Even if only for a second or two, it'll make them stop and think.

Try this: "Pa…pa…pardon, Sir?" Or "Miss-ssssssssssss?"

Pa… pa…pa…pa…paaaar… don, Sir.

Cracking! Using such voices you can question the teacher usually with no danger of a sanction. Questioning him might just get him into a conversation and it's more time out of the lesson.

Then, if you're able, try the Homer Simpson voice, or Mickey Mouse. Watch the reactions of both the teacher and your mates. We'll discuss voices again, later, when we talk about deflecting blame onto someone else. Someone like a nerd, or your mate, or even… the teacher.

Ready to rock and roll? Now, try some funny voices with your neighbour. See if you know who they are.

Three Minutes of Cartoon Voices. Some a Bit Squeaky.

Bit more fun now, folks. After me say "Awwwh".

Awwwh.

Louder.

Awwwh.

Now, Wooo.

Wooo.

Extend that a bit. Wooooooooo.

Wooooooooo.

Now let's see if we can Combo-Rondo. You at the back start with an Awwwh or a Woooo. Quietly. Now the next boy. Now you. In turn. Keep it going. See the effect. No-one's making a big noise, but together it's a real distracter. Altogether, Wooo…

Wooo Woooo Wooooo WOOooooooooooo WOOOOOOOoooooooooo WOOOOOOOOOOOOOOOOOOOOOO!!!!!

Excited Cheering Erupts..

Wooooing. Fun, isn't it? Not only does it get everyone distracted, but even the boffins and nerds start to smile. A teacher faced with 30 smiling faces knows it's a wheeze and will just tell you to calm down and get on with your work. But it can cause a minute or two's break mid-lesson.

So when do you use the *Wooos*? Whenever, the teacher brags about something – teachers shouldn't brag of course but they do now and again (when he scored a try at the weekend). Also, if he unwittingly makes a comment that can be taken two ways, if he awards a fellow pupil a Mars Bar yet makes it sound like a big deal, if he says something that demonstrates his deeper knowledge of his subject. Henry VIII married Anne Boleyn is in all the textbooks, but if he drops in the fact that Anne's aunt's sister was called Clarissa, it might deserve a Wooo or two. Most pupils soon get the hang of it and spot the opportunities as and when they arise.

A similar strategy is humming. But this is rarely done in

sympathy to something the teacher does or says. Humming should be spontaneous and is meant to annoy. One boy begins humming softly, then a second. It's very difficult for the teacher to know who started it. Combo-rondo. Soon the classroom sounds like a nest of hornets. The teacher becomes confused over where it started, who to sanction – and his suspicions that you are ALL taking liberties in his lessons will unsettle him. Mission accomplished. Self-doubt plus a delay.

Some boys make sporadic noises. Like tapping their rulers on the desk. Education theory teaches the teacher not to take this as bad behaviour, but as a sign that a bright child is becoming bored, is ready to learn and needs stretching. So no sanctions. It's annoying but hardly ever gets punished. Now you know that teachers think that way, tap away. If one boy starts to tap, then another, and a third…. it can soon develop into a percussion section.

If you want to push it a bit, if you don't mind risking a short detention, try these. Bring something in that you can bounce that makes a good noise. Ping pong balls are excellent. At first the teacher may think it's a ready-to-learn signal; until he sees what's making the noise. Then let it bounce across the desks of mates, off a wall, onto the floor. Starts a scramble, distracts everyone and stops the teacher in his tracks.

SLIGHT PAUSE.

Teachers sometimes bring it upon themselves by initiating the kinds of silly noise that they dread. If teachers ever crack a joke, don't let them get away with it. Laugh. And laugh and laugh and laugh. Some classes have kept this up for as long as three minutes. A bit of laughter lifts the spirits. A lot of false laughter depresses the teacher. Subtle. "But Miss, it was you that told the joke."

JOKES AND BANTER ARE NATURALLY NOISY.

Teachers like a bit of banter. They feel good about themselves when they come up with creative responses to pupils' comments. Like Mr Godfrey in the *Adverbs Lesson,* teachers get a certain satisfaction from something amusing they've made up on the spare of moment. Even if the teacher's witty remark gives you a better understanding of the topic, it gives you an opportunity to call out. Get a laugh yourself. A series of jokey comments from all over the class can disrupt the flow of the lesson for several minutes. Yes. An example? Huh.

Well in a Maths lesson on fractions, the teacher mentioned integers. When asked what one was the teacher unwisely joked that it might be a wild animal that inhabits the long grass of the Serengeti. This led initially to some false laughter and comments like "good joke, Sir" then to lots of animal comments. And a few beastly noises. Great Combo. The class was still talking Zoology instead of Maths half an hour later.

"I once saw a lesser spotted pythagoras in The West Park". "No, that was a striped pythagoras, Luke, the spotted one has a shorter tail. The lesser pythagoras tends to hang around with hypotenuses". You might even get the teacher joining in.

Of course not all banter involves mythical animals but the wits in the class can play this to the limit. No-one ever gets sanctioned for havin' a laugh. Basically if the teacher cracks a joke, feel free to join in. Noisy lessons are good. They suggest that you are all engaged… engaged in Combos, that is!

Tactic Seventeen - Happy clapping.

Some teacher training colleges cover ways to get a class's attention. These include the teacher lowering his voice, then clapping LOUDLY.

CLAP!

It's likely that he'll clap the once, then when the talking dies down he may clap again, once, maybe twice. This is your cue. After the second clap, you clap. Then your mate next to you. Then a few mates, then everyone. Decrease the time between claps. Soon the whole class is clapping quickly, like those Russian dances. Rapid, happy clapping. Let's practise.

CLAP!
CLAP, CLAP!

Now your turn. Altogether, now.

CLAP... CLAP, CLAP... CLAP, CLAP – CLAP, CLAP.
CONTINUOUS CLAPPING.

Once you've reached a crescendo, everybody cheer. Teachers in adjacent rooms won't fail to notice the clamour through the walls. Your embarrassed teacher won't know which way to turn.

CLAPPING AND CHEERING, FOLLOWED BY LAUGHTER.

TACTIC EIGHTEEN – PHONEY WAR.

Other noisy Combos include the use, OR NOT, of mobile phones. Most schools have a no-phones-during-lessons rule and this then involves the teacher in confiscating your mobile, putting it somewhere safe until the end of the lesson, taking it to the office for you to collect at the end of the day, and so on. Extra work when she's already extra busy. "Well, I was texting him the answer to Question 8", or "I needed to remind Josh that we are catching the same bus" or "my mum texted to say she's not picking me up". So long as it's reasonable. And when she confiscates it, it's also an excuse to interrupt her, to remind her she's got it. Better still, a Combo – ask your mates to ask for it back on your behalf. All leads to extra stress.

Now a really phoney wheeze with your mobiles. Just look down at your lap. You needn't have anything there. Just pretend you are pushing buttons. The teacher might come over. Then, raise your arms and give him a *nothing-here* look. He might peer closely to see if you've dropped something on the floor or passed it to a mate. Again at least a minute lost, and probably also a confused teacher thinking about what's going on instead of Spanish vocabulary. Ole.

TACTIC NINETEEN – WATER, WATER… EVERYWHERE.

No cans in class, no food, but – *worry ye not* – most schools allow water. It's not so sticky and doesn't mess up the desk. Even though it's allowed, the *no drinks in class* rule gives you the opportunity to ask "can I drink water, Sir?" Then someone else must pipe up. "Can I?" And another "And me?" Soon the whole lesson will dissolve into boys opening their bags, taking bottle tops off, dripping and spilling. One boy needing water is worth at least three minutes.

There are times when this can be used as a starter Slo-Pro such as after games. A good PE teacher will give you time after exercising to cool down and take in fluids. The next teacher just sees your red faces, sweaty shirts and gives in to an inevitable few minutes' delay to the Geography lesson.

Mid-lesson a bit of water spilled across the desk, or on the back of the boy in front of you can cause reasonable reactions from your victims. Someone will have to mop it up. And that takes time and can lead to a bit of banter "Sir, he's wet himself again, always doing that". Then that's a good opportunity for an awwww or an ooooh.

For a slightly more risky tactic, pick up a few ice cubes from the fresh fruit counter in the canteen. You'll need a plastic sandwich bag to keep them in, available from all good mothers. Take the ice cubes to your Sociology lesson and just let them melt. On someone else's seat, in the aisle, in the shoe of the guy who likes to do Sociology in his socks. Like a slow fuse they'll prompt a reaction from your fellow pupils and the teacher. Alternatively you could use snowballs, but that's a bit weather dependant.

Tactic Twenty – Loo breaks.

Another water trick. Usually gets a reaction – and a pause in proceedings while teachers work it out. Just casually mention to a male teacher something about the girls' loos, or to a female teacher that the boys' loos are out of operation. A bit of exaggeration helps here.

"Sir, the girls' loos are blocked."

"Miss, the boys' wash basin has cracked itself."

There's nothing they can do about it, well not directly, except stop the lesson to make a note for the caretaker. OK, one-minute chatterbreak now, then we'll talk about how you can practise your legal skills.

BECOME THE CLASS BARRISTER!

Great Combos naturally evolve if you can get into a legitimate argument. Issues can arise during any lesson. Boffins step forward, here. Become the class barrister. Point any issues out. This places the teacher in the role of the judge, which requires time to think – about anything but the main lesson. OK, boffins. Take careful note.

This is a spifferooney. Surreptitiously pretend to open a packet of sweets, crisps or whatever underneath the desk. Your mate then has an excuse to shout out "Miss, he's eating stringy things" followed by someone else saying "Miss, they look like worms". The rest of the class laugh. The teacher must respond, mustn't she?

However, when she comes over just show her an unopened packet "just putting it away, Miss". The teacher now has a problem. Does she speak to you OR to your friend for shouting out? But the friend was trying to help the school, by snitching on a pupil for breaking the rules. Does the teacher let the matter drop; have a go at you; at your mate?

Such tactics create at least a delay of a minute or two, they stop the flow. Even more subtle, any tactic that presents teachers with a dilemma, no matter how trivial, puts them in a situation where they have to make a decision whether to apply school rules or not. The more they think about it, the more self-doubt starts to creep in.

Tactic Twenty-One – Isms.

Teachers are good sorts really. Very fair to everyone. So fair that they get worried at the slightest possibility they've not been. Then there are the legal things about any untoward comment – written or spoken – any misrepresentation, discrimination even.

Teachers need to be careful. But few teachers are legal experts and the law can be complicated. So you can act the class barrister. If anything smacks of unfairness, then question it. Sometimes a teacher, in his urgency to get something underway, may forget a name and refer to a boy by some characteristic. "You, the boy with ginger hair", or "you, with the red bag". Now someone should step in with "Sir, are you gingerphobic; that's gingerism" or "Sir, that's bagism, just 'cause he can't afford a proper leather one". Why not make a few isms up? You can extend the moment if one or two mates join in by agreeing with the original charge. "Old whatisname had to see the Head for calling someone that, Sir". Many NEWTs won't know if you're right or wrong? More experienced teachers won't really fall for this, but they might need to stop a moment to consider your accusation.

140

Tactic Twenty-Two – Equipment breakages.

We've covered how not having equipment can delay the start of a lesson. But it can also present you with some sizzling Combo tactics mid-lesson.

Should your pencil go blunt, your pen run out, your ruler snap, then it's reasonable to stop the flow of the lesson by asking for help… or by starting an argument over a pen. Instead of asking the teacher for a new pen, take one from a mate, or even a nerd if you want to wind him up. But, for argument's sake let's go with the mate. Although for a **real** argument go for the nerd.

You turn around to take your mate's pen. He then calls out "Sir, Sir. He's got my pen." You say "well I needed one, and he's got two." This starts a discussion going which few teachers can ignore. The mate can them come back with another retort. Soon you have a mini court case going on with the teacher the unwitting judge.

An extension of this is the leaky pen. Make sure the ink gets over your hands and the rest of the class see the mess. Now it's time for an "Awwwwwwwh". You ask if you can go to wash your hands making sure that one or two mates share the problem. "Sir, he's got ink all over my book, my desk, my bag."

So far, we've looked at seemingly reasonable interruptions that are unlikely to ever get you into trouble. But what happens if the teacher starts to pay extra attention to your behaviour in particular. Don't panic. When alarm bells start to ring, when a detention is about to be imposed on you… just deflect the blame onto someone else. Onto a nerd, a mate. Even the teacher.

Tactic Twenty-Three – Deflect the blame onto another pupil with (or without) his consent.

Most pupils won't mind you getting them involved in this way as they know what you are up to. Nerdy types deserve to be blamed as it's one of the best ways to get them involved in the Mission. If you and the mate next to you are caught talking, then try this simple diversion. "We WERE talking, but what about the rest of class?"

When you've been caught out and the teacher is about to apply a sanction, have a deflection plan ready. You blame a mate for something. He responds. Teachers have now to intervene to stop the squabbling about this secondary issue and they forget that they were going to sanction you for something else in the first place.

For example, after doing something, like throwing, you can always say "Weren't me, Miss, came from over there." Or "Sir, look what Josh just did."

If the teacher sees you pushing someone, just say that he took your pen, calculator, whatever. Anything to deflect the blame. Then your mate responds and the secondary issue starts. Of course you might both be caught up in a detention, but it was probably worth it – considering the amount of lesson time you've wasted.

Tactic Twenty-Four – Deflect the blame onto the teacher.

Right at the beginning, we discussed how you can slow things down by first saying you have no pen and following this up with "I've asked for a pen, Sir, why won't you give me one?" Followed up by a Combo from your Mate who asks, "Sir, why won't you give him a pen, he needs one?" You slow things down by transferring the blame from you for not having the pen, to the teacher.

Try this. Butt in to say you need help. When the teacher ignores you or tells you to be quiet, you can reasonably comment loudly about this injustice. Either directly to the teacher or to the rest of the class. Then others can join in.

An experienced teacher will have ways of dealing with people who butt in, but NEWTs can get really flustered particularly if it gets back to your parents that one of your new teachers doesn't seem to like you because he refuses to help. You might even let slip that your questions are quite insightful and perhaps he doesn't know the answer.

Tactic Twenty-Five – Deflect the whole issue. Involve another teacher – The Double Bubble.

The Double Bubble, when another teacher is involved. If your teacher asks you to stay behind during break or for 10 minutes at the start of your lunch hour, try the Double-Bubble. Say something like "Sir, Sonny and I already have a sanction with Mrs Awesome". Then start to barter. "Can we do it tomorrow?" "Can we go to Mrs Awesome, now, and come back to you in 15 minutes?" Then the ultimate: "Mrs Awesome will go mad if I don't get there on time."

Seems reasonable. Except your teacher would then have to wait in for an extra 10 minutes for Mrs Awesome's 10-minute detention before he can start his; stopping him from going to his lunch. This can introduce a bit more stress and obviously meets one of our 3Ss. But there's something more subtle. You are effectively telling him that Mrs Awesome's detention is more important than his, or that you're more scared of disobeying Mrs Awesome, undermining his self-respect. If he lets you go to her detention, then self-doubt must start to kick in. If he doesn't, he'll still waste 10 minutes of his lunchtime trying to find Mrs Awesome to check you were telling the truth and to advise her why you didn't turn up. Time-consuming, doubt-inducing, the amazing Double Bubble.

Tactic Twenty-Six – Self-deprecation.

The teacher might tell the class that you can all chat quietly with the boy next to you to discuss the subject. Try this. Lean over, turn around, ignore the boy next to you and ask a boy two rows away. The teacher will likely question this: "Why are you asking him?" You point to the boy next to you and answer "cos he's too thick. John's cleverer". Gets a laugh. Such tactics are rarely sanctioned as you were talking about the work. Gets you respect from John and, so long as the boy next to you is in on it, you get respect from him for slowing down the lesson.

Why are you asking him? 'Cos HE's thick!

This tactic can be extended even further if the boy next to you pretends to take offence to being called thick. By objecting, he is using up more time, involving the teacher to sort out the dispute. It's leading to another very effective Combo.

If you're unlucky, criticising the teacher or other boys might lead to arguments and detentions. But who could possibly be sanctioned for doing themselves down?

If a boy asks a silly question and the teacher ignores him, the boy can then reasonably ask in an exasperating way "why aren't you helping?" "Pleeeeeese help!" "I just don't understand. I'm not feeling very bright, today".

Again, the rest of the class can extend this distraction by saying "Awwwh, Sir, why aren't you helping him?" or "Miss, give him a clue." Or turn it into a general plea with a joint "Pleeeese help him". Again, this Combo transfers the teacher's attention from the primary Mission tactician to the whole class and usually dilutes the teacher's willingness to sanction.

Tactic Twenty-Seven – Playground Combos.

When they can't work it out, there starts the self-doubt.

A confused teacher is an ineffective one; if they don't understand what's going on, how can they react? In their classroom, they might question what is going on; but in the playground, well, the teaching textbooks and University lectures just don't cover ways for teachers to cope with these rather subtle tactics. Here's two to confuse even the most experienced teacher. Before school be *statuesque*, after school *energise*.

This first playground tactic is most effective for boys who use an early bus. Whatever the day, whatever the weather, if you are in the school grounds around 8am just stand around, expressionless, gazing into space. Like statues. Don't play football, don't jump around. Just stand in silence. You can do it alone. Or as a Combo in twos and threes, but stand still and don't talk. Even better, if it's raining. Teachers might comment that you are getting wet or may utter a wary "morning", but they will rarely intervene. Most will just walk past as if you weren't there, but at the back of their minds they know that playgrounds are for running around on. That's what boys do. That's what teachers expect. Do something unexpected, act like statues; you'll get them thinking.

After school, do the opposite. Adults may expect you to be worn out after concentrating for five or six lessons, particularly if you've had double French or Science. The French and Science teachers certainly are. No time now for standing around. Push, shove. Bounce around like dogs off a lead. Jump on each other's backs. The teachers in the playground at this time will invariably be on bus duty. They don't want to be there. They've got lessons to plan, parents to phone about your behaviour, marking to do, meetings to go to. Why should they give up 20 minutes to see you on the bus? Think of Mr Godfrey's hectic day and you'll get the point. It's the last place he wants to be. And if you are running around, shouting and bouncing, you'll have them looking everywhere at once to see if they need to break something up. Pretend fights (with a smile) can be most effective.

As the bus approaches, stand in a neat line. That's basic health and safety. But as soon as it stops, try rushing the door. A bit of untidy queuing, the odd shove and push will get a teacher's attention. It's one thing more for him to worry about. The ultimate is having so many boys stepping onto the bus at once, that you all get stuck in the door.

Once on the bus. Relax. Day's job done. If you look back out of the window, you'll see several teachers making their slow walk back to the building, heads down, shoulders hunched, wondering where all your energy came from. They still have an hour or two at school followed by two hours at home marking. And if it's raining, so much the better. They'll have to sit in their classroom or in a school meeting, dripping wet.

Tactic Twenty-Eight – When we gotta get outta this place.

Some days you'll be thoroughly fed up with a lesson. It'll be a case of 'we gotta get out of this place if it's the last thing we ever do' *(ADVP breaks into song, vaguely resembling something by The Animals)*.

You are worn out. You may have been up all night playing computer games or just feeling tired out from double Maths. By the middle of the morning you'll be totally bored, you'll just want to get out of the room. Midway through a lesson. But many schools stipulate that once you're in a classroom, you're in for the duration. A teacher shouldn't take any notice of any plea for you to leave. So, how can you get excused mid-lesson?

We referred to **"The runny pen trick"** earlier. Everyone knows that pens kept in your pocket or on hot pipes are likely to run a bit. Teachers just can't say "No" to a request to leave the room if you have a hand covered in messy ink. They can't afford to let it get smeared all over the desks, textbooks or the backs of the shirts of other boys. With NEWTs, consider this as an invitation for a walkabout down the corridor or an opportunity to spend five or ten minutes in the washrooms. More experienced teachers may stipulate a time constraint: "make sure you're back in two minutes". But they rarely check the clock. Whatever, not only have your messy comments got everyone woooing and you've stopped the flow of the lesson, you've knocked a few minutes off for everyone, but now – as you leave the room – you can involve one or two others by pretending to put your hand down all over whatever they're working on. Then when you eventually return to the lesson, you can go for the bonus – leave it one or two minutes and then pipe up "Sir, got no pen!"

Another excuse to leave the room is the old favourite **"My mate's ill"**. Most schools have a quiet room for pupils who don't feel too well. If YOU want to get out then just look around the room for a mate who's looking a bit peaky. Then point him out to the teacher. "Sir, Joe's ill. I'd better take him to see the nurse." When the teacher says that he can go on his own, try something like "Sir, I'd better help him. He's really wobbly" or "He doesn't know where to go". The rest of the class can come in with "Yes, Sir, he's Joe's best mate. He should take him." Rather than waste any more time on your interruptions, many teachers will say "go on then", and you're outta there. But make sure the patient walks ever so jittery and slowly to the door.

Well now, boys, the VP is gesturing. Seems it's nearly time for me to get outta here. Think he wants to give you a bit of feedback on the Adverbs lesson. Pass you back to the VP now. See you tomorrow. Afternoon everybody.

GOOD AFTERNOON, SIR [IN CHORUS.]

PLENARY.

Thank you ADVP. Well done, gentlemen. Settle now quickly. Quick-**lee**. Adverb. So, let's summarise. Today we looked at

Combos and discussed how a good Combo can get you off the hook from sanctions, at least the horrible ones. We considered how teachers try to plan lessons to the minute. And you demonstrated how with just a few tactics, even with little practice, you could shorten the productive parts of a lesson by up to a third.

Well, WELL, as a first attempt at Mission tactics most of you did rather WELL. One or two things we can tidy up, but on the whole not bad. Your expertise in the use of Mission tactics should grow over the years, you'll refine your approach each time you try one out; you'll learn from each other. Practice makes perfect.

Tomorrow first thing, I'll have the reports back from the three teachers plus their observers. There will be prizes, so that should be something extra to look forward to.

YESSSSSSS!

But that's for tomorrow. We've over-run a bit in the MTPS, so we've just a little time for your questions on any aspect of today's programme.

Any questions about the practice lesson? No, next question, please.

I got 33, Sir. When do I get my reward?

There was no reward. We were only practising.

Sir!

Oh go on. Godfrey, give him a Mars Bar.

That's unfair, Sir. He wasn't helping the Mission. He was being a show-off trying to get all the answers.

Yes, Sir, it's unfair.

It's not what you've told us to do.

STOP! Now! Another question. Over there. Speak up, now.

QUIET ASIDE
See, VP. Can they really be trusted?

Sir, who writes these books telling teachers how we should behave? Are they stern? Are they really good teachers?

Good teachers? Can you imagine any good teacher would give up teaching to write books? Inexperienced teachers regularly suffer low-level disruption, but equally do not know how to counteract it. Sterner teachers with perfect class control probably do have the answers, but they have less experience of it happening so would have less to write about. Catch 22. Anyway, no full-time teacher has time to write books.

Bet Heads write them?

Heads generally don't experience really bad behaviour in their classes. Boys don't misbehave when the Head is around. Like a policeman on the motorway seldom sees anyone doing over 70mph, Heads rarely see anyone breaking the rules. These Heads will confidently tell your parents that there is hardly any bad behaviour in their schools. Not with the behaviour management systems they have in place. Few Heads write a book while they are Heads.

Must be experts, Sir, who writes them? Experts.

In life, in general, be careful when it comes to experts. How did they become experts? Have they ever taught in tough schools? The Mission is wary of such types, but thankfully for us a lot of experts that give talks to teachers about child psychology and how to apply it to teaching don't actually teach; they've long ago given up teaching to concentrate on what they consider to be a more intellectually challenging academic career. Wonder why.

Is there a book we can get on Mission tactics, Sir? For the Mission?

Hope not! *[FROM SIDE OF ROOM]*

Godfreee?

No, gentlemen. Our tactics are passed on only by word-of-mouth. Saves a lot of reading, which is how most boys prefer it. I'll take no more questions? Let's leave five minutes earlier today, as you worked so well in the SloPro exercise. See you all tomorrow, gentlemen. And remember, to look around as you leave. Front row first this time. Single file. Off you go.

CHATTERING AND CLATTERING, STOMPING STEPS, JAUNTY, REGGAE BACKGROUND MUSIC.

What are you doing?

Writing, Sir. Just finishing off the essay… wanted a Mars Bar, Sir.

Go on, leave. Go home!

The strains of Bob Marley's 'You Can't Blame The Youth' drowns the rest of this conversation.

WHISPERED.
Major General was spot on as usual, Godfrey. Don't you agree? Such over-diligent note-taking… can't risk things getting out. Better call a Staff Meeting.

Day Four.

Everyone agrees that teachers are Outstanding. Revealed – the secret rooms in every school. The boys reluctantly do a bit of Maths.

Thursday, Lesson 1
Commotion Combos.

I can see that some of you are a little excited this morning. After your lesson on Adjectives and Adverbs. Do you want to know how you got on?

YEAAAAH!

Thank you. Settle down.

Well, as a first attempt at Mission tactics, gentlemen, most of you did rather well. One or two things we can tidy up, but on the whole not bad. As we said right at the start, your expertise in the use of Mission tactics should grow over the years, you'll refine your approach each time you try one out; you'll learn from each other. Practice makes perfect.

Of course by now all of you boys should recognise a Mission tactic when someone starts one off; these things seem to come naturally. But some of you looked as though you were a little reticent at the start of yesterday's practice lesson. Quite natural, but no need to worry. If you find it hard to get involved in the first term in Year 7, then watch carefully for the early adopters. A few shone yesterday. And it's these boys that we really want to reward today.

But first there's a mention for the person who obtained the most marks on the worksheets – Mantoni, you're a right little boffin. But high marks for English wasn't the main purpose of the exercise. So, no prizes today, Mantoni.

Special rewards go to Plumb in Mrs Benyana's class, Asif in Mr Godfrey's class, Williams-Jones in Mr Higginbotham's lesson and Bilko in Mrs Shah's. YOU were the real heroes. Come to the front, please. Quickly, please.

SHUFFLING FOLLOWED BY APPLAUSE.

Thank you, gentlemen. These four boys each started at least one tactic during the lesson, but it was the way that they supported the others that impressed us. Stand up straight, please. Take pride. Respect.

Their actions always seemed reasonable and Mrs Benyana felt that Plumb was actually trying to be helpful, which on his first attempt at a tactic was remarkably good. We all knew that Plumb wasn't trying to be helpful, especially when he dropped her books, but she didn't cotton on.

We'd like to give you four boys special Summer Skool medals but as there's a danger your parents might find them and be alerted to the Summer Skool, we've disguised them a bit. No mention of the school, but if you look closely, you'll see the 3S Mission logo.

Other boys tried very hard and they too will receive treats. Again we must keep these away from parents, so for these boys we've chosen prizes that, as in the best spy movies, can be studied carefully and then consumed. Prize winners' names are on the board over there. You can collect them shortly after the next exciting episode of Combos. Back to you, ADVP.

Go, Go – Combo

Bump.!

Well what a nice surprise – special medals. You can all earn these if you show your mettle. Mettle, mind – don't show your medal, ha. Metal, medal even.

Not Very Convincing Laughter.

Mr Assistant Deputy, Sir, that's pants.

Oh, well, not here to joke, we're moving onto seriously creative Combos today. Good to go, are we? So far we've suggested one or two things to start things off, backed up by one or two responses from your mates. These next Combos require close coordination and depend upon your quick wittedness on the day. We call them *Commotion Combos*. Here, the permutations of who says what and when are almost limitless. So every Commotion Combo will be slightly different and will develop an energy of its own. But you'll get the gist. And YOU will be the creative force. Exciting, eh? Energy goes hand in hand with movement – and movement can be devastating!

Did I say "movement"? Up on your feet. Everyone stand up. Reach for the sky. Both arms. As high as you can. Now, without banging your heads on the desk, touch your toes. And again. Once more. Do it ten times.

Now stretch your right arm out and try to tap the nearest boy on the shoulder. Stretch. Strrrrrretch! Good.

CHUCKLING. SOUND OF BOYS TOPPLING SIDEWAYS.

Now the left arm. The more you do this the longer your arms become. In the olden days, before computer games, this was a popular playground activity. See how long your arms can become. OK… and relax.

LAUGHTER AND CHATTER.

Good, all warmed up for some creative thinking. This lesson you'll find yourselves developing something new, something beautifully original; teamwork and camaraderie will come into it. Most enjoyable… and you'll get better and better with practice.

TACTIC TWENTY-NINE – BE A BORROWER.

If nothing else, Summer Skool wants to teach you to be good and reasonable, always. We have our principles. Most boys stick to them and are excellent Mission Musketeers. So here's a valuable lesson. NEVER steal from a teacher, NEVER steal from a fellow pupil, NEVER take things that aren't yours away from school. EVER! In all our years in schools, we've found that the vast majority of children follow this key principle. Stealing makes you feel bad about yourselves; no-one likes a thief.

So NEVER take things from school. EVER! However, no harm really in borrowing the odd item or two – especially from the teacher's desk. So move things around the classroom but you must never take them from the room. We spoke about borrowing the teacher's textbook on Monday. But then you had an excuse as you could say you needed it for your work. But sometimes you might want to borrow something just out of curiosity, no more.

Borrow the teacher's papers, the interactive board pen, his results sheet, any resource you think he might be planning to impose on you – all are fair game. If he's brought in something special to help him to demonstrate a particular point and the thing is not too big, just borrow it. While a boffin distracts his attention away from his desk, the boy on the front row can take the object or paper and pass it under the desk to the guy behind. He must do this quickly so that if the teacher thinks he's spotted something and questions the front row boy, then the boy can hold his hands up, stand up, move away from his desk and protest his innocence in the knowledge that the borrowed object is now back around row three. The boy next to him can help here by supporting his mate with "he did nothing, Sir, give him a break". The accused can even pretend to help the teacher by looking through the pile of papers on the teacher's desk.

Eventually someone can drop it into a corner or on a windowsill behind the blinds. The next person to see it will probably be the caretaker when he does his evening round.

If a teacher spots someone moving around at the back and looks as though he's coming to investigate, just say "How can I have taken it when I'm at the back? My arms aren't that long". Gets a laugh and diffuses a potentially tricky moment.

TACTIC THIRTY – GO WALK ABOUT.

Teachers need order to conduct an effective lesson. Commotion Combos are all about movement and while movement is important in drama and dance lessons, in most other classes being dynamic is sheer dynamite!

Art or Science might need you to move around to get your brushes or equipment for an experiment. But these lessons are usually conducted in large rooms with large tables. During Maths or an English lesson, History or Geography – any subject taught in a small room – then walking about will freak 'em out.

Freak 'em out. Walk about.

Just think about it. If you were a teacher. Pupils walking around the room, standing in front of you, standing behind you, fiddling with your computer, your board pens… all causes confusion, a loss of control. If more than one pupil is involved then the teacher won't know which way to look – behind him at the side, straight ahead. No idea what is going on. Stress and self-doubt will creep in. Year 7s have an ideal excuse. In Primary school they will have been used to walking about to get glue or a ruler or some other equipment. Primary teachers usually plan for this and anyway the pupils are quite small. But at Secondary school if you have five or six boys taller than the teacher moving about, it's a major stressor.

Now we've all come across the odd lad who just can't sit still. He needs to stretch his legs – he can't help it; he was born that way – fidgety. And leggy. Often out of his seat, he stands up and down, tips back on his chair, falls over sideways. Somehow he gets his legs to stray under, or over, the desk – kicking the boys in front, distracting everyone around him. Teachers are aware of such types and often give them the benefit of the doubt. If you have a Tommy-longlegs in your class, then by all means use his distractions to get up to other tactics.

Equally look for excuses for YOU to be out of your place. Remember, look for reasonable excuses. Movement can start with one person, possibly a boffin rushing out to ask for extra work. Or just someone taking a quiet stroll down the aisle. "Where are you going?" "Dunno", then sit down. Never gets a sanction. Often gets a laugh. Always gets the teacher wondering.

Any excuse to move around. Appear helpful. Walk over to another boy saying "Just showing him". Or appear sympathetic to a fellow pupil's needs: "I was just seeing if he was alright. Have to look after your mates".

Conversely, look out for useful conflict situations. Start grabbing at the boy next to you. "He stole my calculator. Sir, just getting it back". Your mate then pushes back. You retort with an obviously exaggerated claim "Arrgh, he broke meee arm, Sir. What are you going to do about it, Sir?"

Oh, and if the teacher ever asks a boy to approach the front, like "come out with your homework", then lots of boys might go up and crowd around the teacher's desk with their homework pages open, demonstrating how keen they are, yet really causing confusion and blocking the teacher's view from whatever else is going on in the room. Meanwhile Tommy longlegs has them wrapped around someone's neck at the back.

Tactic Thirty-One – Blinds panic.

Open the windows, lower the blinds. It's hot. It's cold. Such opportunities. There seems to be a psychological need for boys sitting next to windows to want to play with those cord things. And no-one – certainly no adult I know – can work out which cord to pull to make the blinds go up or down. So, when told not to fiddle with them, just say "Sir, can I shut out the sun?" or "can I open the window?" Then struggle a bit. Distracts those around you, diverts the teacher's attention away from the lesson, yet rarely gets a sanction.

But there's more; that boy Justus brought this one to our attention yesterday. The further away you are from the window, the better. Someone two rows away can ask for air. The boy next to the window must indicate that he doesn't want to involve himself with the window by offering a reasonable excuse "I'm busy, Sir, on Question 17". Now the person who asked has a great excuse to leave his desk, climb over the boy in the window seat and halt the lesson for two or three minutes.

And once a window is open, then magically pencil cases and rulers seem to be sucked through them onto any Year 7 pupils passing by below.

Tactic Thirty-Two – Games.

Teachers like you to enjoy their lessons. So long as it's their kind of fun. Prearrange the occasional Combo game to lighten up a particularly boring lesson. Here's a few snorters.

We mentioned Bingo yesterday – most teachers, particularly the older ones have regular catch phrases they use during lessons. Phrases like "No, Alex, **NOOOOOOOOOO!**" or "not really clever that, Mitchell" or "you didn't **really** mean that did you, Patel?" or "you're not looking, Wes". Every teacher does it; every teacher has different expressions they use most lessons. They don't even know they're saying them half the time.

Then there are the open questions – "Why can't you do as you are told? ", "Why have you no pen?" Were you raised in a barn?" "How many times have I asked you to…?" Lots of opportunities for you to shout out an answer: or another question "how was such a thing silly, Sir?"

So, Bingo. Before the lesson, everyone chooses any six of the target teacher's favourite phrases and writes them on a blank sheet, or even at the back of their exercise books. Whenever a phrase you've selected comes up, cross it off your list. The first to hear the six he's chosen, stands up and shouts "Bingo". He might get a detention, but he'll get a lot of respect from the others, and the teacher will start to wonder if perhaps he's using some expressions too much. More self-doubt.

Here's another whole class game. While the teacher has his back half turned, one boy stands up then quickly sits down. Then the next. Soon a Mexican wave develops. As it reaches its peak, the teacher will look around, scratching his head in amazement, the class whooping and cheering. Remember whole class detentions are frowned upon, so what can he do? Just let it go; after all you're all enjoying yourselves.

A derivation of this is *Shark* in which one boy raises an arm like he's swimming, then brings the arm down to his mouth and pretends to be yawning, then another at the other side of the room, then another. The tenth boy raises his arm and shouts "Shark". Now if the teacher spots this midway, then that person is out for the next round until someone who shouts "Shark" wins. Just make sure you've counted correctly. And as the ninth arm goes down watch very closely as you can be sure several boys will be competing to win.

Bit more brain gym now. Starting with you in the corner, let's play Shark. Go. Now!

SHUFFLING.

Shark!

161

Merriment.
More Shuffling.

Shhhhh… shark.

One at once, please, but you get the drift. Good game, eh?

Tactic Thirty-Three – Time's not right.

Here's another trick for a Tommy longlegs. Before the lesson, someone – usually one of the taller lads – takes the classroom clock down off the wall just for a few seconds and hands it to the smallest guy in the class. He puts the clock fast by five minutes. Towards the end of the lesson, everyone can start to pack up five minutes before the teacher asks you to. Someone say "Miss, it's time to go" and point at the clock. Others can join in. You might even start to get up and walk towards the door. If the teacher questions this by saying "Wait for the bell" everyone in chorus can say "bell's been wrong all week". Someone might add something like "been out ever since the Ofsted fire alarm prank last month" or "didn't you get the email" or some other excuse that involves a bit of technology.

At worst you waste four minutes arguing, at best you get out five minutes early. If the teacher suspects clock tampering, then the tall guy can truthfully say "didn't change it, Miss" and the smallest guy couldn't possibly have reached up there.

Tactic Thirty-Four – The 'Bell Rush'.

One step on from the clock watching, is the Bell Rush. Now if you've implemented a few Mission tactics to slow things down, then it goes without saying that the teacher will be struggling for time at the end of a lesson. He probably won't have time for his Plenary – but that probably doesn't matter as most teachers only fully employ them when Ofsted are around. Nor will he have time to present the flourishing finish that he'd planned. So he'll be in mid-sentence just as the bell goes. You will have already packed your things in your bag bit by bit during the previous five minutes. This is standard practice. But now as soon as the bell goes you rush the door. All of you! The teacher will stand in your way and tell you to get back, but you just stand there facing him. You can't turn around because others are joining the scramble. One or two boys might try to prise through the door crying "Ouch, he's pushing me". The teacher can either wait until you all return to your seats or give up and let you all through the door. You might think that an experienced teacher might stand his ground, but not always. After all it was his fault he didn't finish the lesson. Already flustered by this, disappointed that he didn't get in that flourishing ending and faced in a stand-off by 30 pupils, he is likely to need a break more than ever. Half the time he'll stand his ground; the other half he'll say "Go on then, off you go." The object of the Bell Rush isn't to get you to break early. It's a very effective stressor that will test your teacher's resolve not to break early. And then you've accomplished all three Mission targets.

The Bell Rush tactic may take a few goes before you perfect it. A single rusher won't work; needs at least four or five to go on the B of the bell, followed quickly by the rest. Rugby players are particularly good at the Bell Rush.

So there we have it. That's Commotion Combos. Some super-dooper, razzle-dazzlers. One big message as I too rush for the door. Go, go Combo!

Thanks, ADVP. Commotion Combo tactics are excellent for NEWTs, particularly those that have just finished their behaviour management courses. They'll think they'll be ready for you, gentlemen. They've been trained to deal with you. They've confidence in their new skills, but they've been trained mainly to handle one pupil at a time. Once they are faced with several boys in unison, they start to doubt everything they ever learned at university about behaviour management. They doubt that they should ever have come into teaching and start to look for alternative careers. Let's help them on their way.

Short break while the prize winners come forward, the rest of you can relax for five minutes, then we'll slow things down a bit. With a bit of Maths.

Urrgh!

Quiet, PLEASE, gentlemen.

QUIET, THEN FOOTSTEPS, THEN GENERAL CHATTER.

Thursday, Lesson 2
Prime Factors – the Plan.

Thank you ADVP. Well done, prize winners. Eat them at break or at home. Not now. YOU… that wrapper. Pick it up.

OK, next lesson, gentlemen, just after your break, once again we'll go straight to the Mission Tactic Practice Suites. Look out for the lists of names on the board. They'll show you which of the four classes you're in. We've moved people around to get you to practise Combos off the cuff, no matter who you're sharing the lesson with. This next *Tactics Practice* lesson will be on Maths…

No, Nooooooooooo.

Thank you. Don't panic. You're not here to learn the Maths. Just to practise the tactics. Particularly mid-lesson. We'll let the lesson flow for the first 15 minutes. Then midway, I'll blow the whistle; then you can let rip with any of the tactics we've covered so far. OK? Once again, we have several real teachers to practise on; all taken from our pool of teachers who need to earn a bit of extra money over the summer holidays. This is Mr Godfrey's lesson plan for a Maths lesson on Prime Factors.

Thought he was an English teacher.

Thank you. Please don't shout out. Like most teachers, Mr Godfrey is multifaceted – expected by their schools to have a go at teaching nearly everything, at least to you younger classes.

Eyes up. At the board. Look. NOW! Here's his lesson objectives and a very detailed plan outlining what he will do, and what he expects from you, minute by minute. I won't read it all out, but we should note his objectives and one or two of the times that he's specially marked.

Prime Factors

LEARNING OBJECTIVES
- **By the close of this lesson, I should be able to:**
- **Understand what factors are (Level 4)**
- **Understand what prime numbers are (L 4)**
- **Use Factor Trees to find Prime Factors (L 5)**
- **Express PFs in index form (Extension – L 6)**

Again, Mr Godfrey has listed certain actions at certain times. For example, here at 12.15 you'll see that Mr Godfrey has put two asterisks. These remind him to discuss famous books about spies. Although this has little to do with Maths, it introduces a bit of literacy and may encourage some of you to pick up an Ian Fleming book. Schools like these *cross curricular activities*. Ofsted likes these. So Heads like them. During Maths lessons, boys like them 'cause it's less Maths to do. Girls like them because it's about reading and they like reading. For teachers, it's a win-win situation all round.

As with the English lesson, yesterday, Mr Godfrey has worked in a number of opportunities to assess your work. At 12.17 he's going to come up with 20 questions for you to work on in pairs. He wants everyone to complete the first 16 questions. These start easy and work up to Level 5. Then he's included three or four Level 6 questions for the boffins, with a note for him to discuss index form with them.

Here's a slide of the worksheet. You'll see a list of numbers from 1 to 30 and an instruction saying *"to find the prime numbers, cross out any number that can be divided by any smaller number and circle what's left. The circled numbers are your primes"*. It's something he'll discuss further with you during the lesson.

CLICK!

And here's a slide of a *Factor Tree*. You'll get what it's all about during the lesson and how to use them to find *Prime Factors*. There are about 30 problems for you to work on, if it all goes to plan.

Mr Godfrey, Mrs Benyana, Mrs Shah and Mr Higginbotham will meet you in the Mission Tactic Practice Suites at 12 noon to deliver the lesson. Remember, today we are practising mid-lesson tactics. So, gentlemen, you must let Mr Godfrey introduce the topic and go along with him for the first 20 minutes or so. Then, when we tell you, start your tactics. Combos get extra marks. Commotion Combos the most marks. Any questions?

GLEEFUL MURMURING IN ANTICIPATION.

Off to your break now. There's an extra 10 minutes to work out some Combos with your mates. Take a look at the class lists, note your room and which teacher you are in with, and as you enter the MTPS you will each be given a box with equipment such as rulers and pencils. Best of luck. Front row first this time. Single file. Off you go. See you in the MTPS sharp at high noon.

Stop worrying, Godfrey. Fully in hand, after last night's staff meeting… for Friday. Agree with the Major General. Can't let things get out, like that. No need to concern yourself. We have ways to easily get shut of them. You just get ready with your prime numbers.

Using Factor Trees to find Prime Factors
A lesson given by Mr Godfrey

CHATTERING, FOLLOWED BY FOOTSTEPS. THEN QUIET.

Good afternoon, lads. Had a good break?

Yes, Mr Godfrey... Sir. [IN UNISON]

Please come in. On your desks you will find a worksheet with all the numbers from two to 30.

SHUFFLING INTO PLACE.

We are going to sort out the prime numbers. Anyone know what a prime number is?

NO RESPONSE.

Well some numbers have *factors*, that's numbers that divide into them. Like 32 can be divided by the numbers four and eight. But some numbers can only be divided by the number one and themselves. No other number goes into them. We call these *prime numbers*. For example seven and eleven. Now take a look at that worksheet. On it are all the numbers from two to 30. We are going to cross out any number that a smaller number will go into. Let's do one together – the number 12. Who can tell me any smaller number that goes into 12? Yes, you at the side over there.

Four goes into 12, Sir.

Well done. Any others?

Sir, and the number three goes into 12 as well.

Fine fellow! We can cross out twelve. As I said, these smaller numbers, like three and four, have a special name. They're called factors of 12. Can someone find me another number that has factors, smaller numbers that go into it?

Easy, this, Eight! Four goes into it.
And nine. Three goes into nine.

Glad you're finding it easy. OK look at the sheets, lads, and find me some more numbers. Cross 'em out. While you are doing that, could you on the front row please hand out these textbooks, one between two? Thank you, what's your name?

INDISTINCT REPLY.

Carry on… and while I log you all in the register, I want you to cross out every other number up to 30 that has factors. First to finish put your hand up. You should end up with a lot of numbers crossed out, but a few won't be. You can circle these.

QUIET, PUNCTUATED BY MR GODFREY CALLING OUT THE
NAMES AND BOYS ANSWERING "YES, SIR" OR "HERE, SIR" AND

Yes, anyone finished? What's your name?

Goodridge, Sir.

Well done. Finished first? Excellent! Good fellow.

His name isn't Goodfellow, it's Goodridge, Sir.

Thank you. Smart… fellow! Now Goodridge, which numbers on your sheet haven't been crossed out?

Sir, there's two and three and five and seven.

Someone else carry on from seven…

Do we write down the two little numbers that make the big number?

No need really, Suresh, but you can if it helps you. I'm looking for any numbers that haven't been crossed out.

Sir, got no pen. It's run out.

Well catch it before it gets any further, laddie.

Funneee, Sir.

Stop right there!

Vice Principal?

Sorry, Godfrey, sorry to butt in from the back. We did say that we don't want to see any SloPros just yet. Otherwise we'll never get to the part of the lesson where we can practise your mid-lesson Combos. That was a good pen tactic yesterday, gentlemen. Today you have to wait for my signal. I'll give you a loud whistle when I want you to start. Not before! Mr Godfrey, please proceed.

Thank you Vice-Principal.

Good! OK. Pens down. Let's see what we've found. After seven, the next number not to be crossed out should be... anyone? *(MURMUR)* Correct it's 11. You over there, you don't look too sure, check with the boy next to you.

Sir, Sir.

YES?

I really don't have a pen, Sir.

Borrow one, lad.

Can anyone give me the next three unchecked numbers? You, please.

SHUFFLING.

Thank you. Good to see you handing out the books so efficiently... and with a smile. OK, you again, can you give me your next three unchecked numbers?

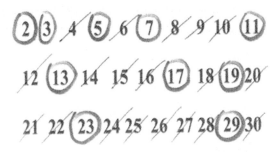

Sir, Sir, my next three circled numbers are 13, 17 and 21.

Good, lad. Well nearly. Anyone spot his mistake?

Seven goes into 21, Sir. He should have crossed it out.

Everyone seems to be getting the idea. Here on the board, crossed out, are all the numbers that smaller factors go into. And, the circled numbers, the ones you couldn't cross out are the special, prime numbers and they are very useful in Mathematics. Anyone know why?

QUIET.

Lots of reasons. Here's one.

CLICK!!

Can anyone tell me who this is? You, second row. Thank you.

James Bond, Sir.

Yes, James Bond. MI6's master spy. Prime numbers are used a lot in code-breaking and secret messages used by super spies like James Bond. And who's this?

SILENCE.

He's called John Le Carre and he wrote a famous book called *The Spy Who came in from The Cold*.

Bit of literacy for you, ah, tick. Quickly back to the Maths. As I said, the small numbers that go into bigger ones are called factors. If the small number itself is a prime number, then it is called a *Prime Factor*. Can anyone give me prime numbers that are factors of 12? Yes, you at the side.

Two and three, Sir, both go into 12.

Good, Desmond, two and three are the Prime Factors of 12. What about four? Is that a prime factor?

No, Sir, it's even. Two goes into four; four's not a prime.

Well done; now copy out these learning objectives for the main lesson. On the board, now. Come on. Two minutes to write them down, then I'll continue.

RELATIVE QUIET, SCRIBBLING.

Good, everyone finished? So far, we've looked at numbers up to 30. Pens down. Everyone look up now at the board. NOW, thank you! Now, what about much bigger numbers? Like 2,345,568?

What do we need to do to tell if it's a prime?

If a smaller number goes into it, Sir.

Well done. Can you think of any small numbers that go into it?

Well let's start by seeing if it will divide by one of the smaller primes like two, three or five.

YOU, stop that yacking at the back!

How do you know if a big number can be divided by a two, or three or five – just by looking at it? Well, if it's EVEN you can divide it by two; anything ending in a five or a zero divides by five. Now what about numbers three goes into? All numbers, no matter how long, whose digits add up to a multiple of three can be divided by three.

Anyone like to have a go with 2,345,568?

Sir. That long millions number was even. Two goes into it.

Easy isn't it?

And three, Sir! 2 + 3+ 4 + 5 + 5 + 6 + 8 adds up to 33 which is a multiple of three.

Yes, boffin (sigh). Now we'll turn to page 53 and look at some really big numbers in question 5A. Just write down which small prime goes into each number.

ODD COUGH. RELATIVE QUIET. THE BOYS WORK QUIETLY FOR 10 MINUTES ON Q5.

OK. Well done, lads. Let's recap. Each of these numbers that goes into another is called a... all together.

Factor. [ONLY A FEW VOICES]

And any factor that's also a prime number is called a...

Prime factor! [MORE VOICES]
Is it like the X-Factor, Sir?

No, lad! Wherever you get an x – that would be algebra.

Booo. Algebra, Sir. Booo!
Booooooooo. [COLLECTIVE BOOING]

Thank you. Settle down. In this lesson you are going to learn a simple, systematic way to work out all the prime factors of big numbers. Some of them really big. Really, really big. Like billions.

But we'll start with something small-ish like 24. To do this we write 24 at the top of our page in a box like this. You do it, now. To start, we want two numbers that multiplied together give us 24. Any offers? You by the window...

Three eights make 24, Mr Godfrey.

Stout fellow. So now from the bottom of the box we put two lines, one going to an eight, the other to a three. These are the factors. Is either a prime number?

Yes, three is. So we put a circle around the three. Now that leaves the eight. It's not a prime, so we carry on splitting it until we reach a prime. Can you tell me two numbers that multiply together to make eight? Put two lines from the eight and write down these two factors.

Two and four, Sir.

Good. Which of these is a prime?

That's right, the two. Circle it. That leaves the four not circled. What goes into four?

Two times two equals four, Sir.

Mr Godfrey in his prime.

So everyone draw two little branch lines from the four and put a two at the end of each line… and as these twos are primes we can circle them.

Now list in numerical order all the numbers circled and put a times sign between them. What have you got?

Two times two times two times three.

Correct – 2 X 2 X 2 X 3

And that is the way you show the prime factors of 24. What's more, it doesn't matter which two numbers you choose to multiply together at the start, you end up with the same prime factors.

Sir, two times 12 also gives 24.

And when you go through the process you still end up circling three 2s and one 3 for 24.

We'll do one more example together – a bit harder – then you can have a go in pairs with your neighbour at some massive numbers.

Let's see, a big number… like 98.

First put 98 in a box, draw two lines from the box and write in two factors. Tell me two numbers that make 98.

Bemused Silence.

Is 98, odd or even?

Even, Sir.

So what goes into it?

Two!

How many times? Divide 98 by two.

*We don't really learn division at primary anymore.
My granddad did it.*

Where's that boffin?

*Two times 49 makes 98. Sir, I have two at the end of one line
and 49 the other one.*

Good man, well done. Learn your times tables when you're young,
like him, and you too will see the patterns numbers make. Tables are
not just for multiplying. Times tables are also key when dividing.

Now, anyone else, will anything go into 49?

SILENCE.

YOU... Don't just sit there, work it out. Come on, 49 is a well-
known multiple.

WHISTLE FROM BACK!

Yes, Vice Principal?
    OK, gentlemen, you may now start your mid-lesson Combos.
    Lads. Quick. Quickly, concentrate – what number goes into
49? Think squares.

Trafalgar Square, Sir?

Try the number seven squared. So now we have 98 at the top, with two branch lines with a 49 and a two at the end of them. The two is circled as it's a prime. From the 49 we have branches to two sevens, both circled. This tells us that the prime factors of 98 are two times seven times seven.

$2 \times 7 \times 7 = 98$

We call these diagrams with circles and branches *Factor Trees*. Now have a go by yourselves. Turn to page…

My dad works in a factoreeeeeee., Sir.

LAUGHTER.

Not very clever, lad. Please let that be the last time you interrupt the class's work. Now please, everyone go to page 53 and have a go at exercise 9C, all the questions up to 20. Work with the lad next to you. Put each big number in a box at the top and construct a factor tree.

No pen, Sir.

WHIZZZZ.

Do we use a pen to draw the tree, or a pencil?

Either, just get on with it. You've got ten minutes. Then we'll check how far you've got. TEN minutes.

Sir, we don't have page 53. It's missing.

Let me look. What? Don't be silly. You'll be the first I ask for an answer. Get on!

QUIET. SOFT FOOTSTEPS.

Aa..aaa..gh, not AGAIN! Which of you left that bag there?

KICKING SOUND.

Sir, I've got eggs in that.

Stop yoking, young man!

LAUGHTER, AT FIRST FROM ONE CORNER, THEN ACROSS ROOM, RISING TO A CRESCENDO OF FALSE GUFFAWING. LASTS ABOUT TWO MINUTES.

Let's get on now, please. Hand up, over there. Yes?

SHUFFLING. FOOTSTEPS.

Let's see. Yes, that bit's correct. But which two numbers multiply to make that?

Sir, he's wet himself!
Awwwh! Awwwh, Sir!

Put that water bottle away. Wipe it up. NOW!

No tissues, Sir.

Come out, there's a cloth on my desk.

Sounds of a Struggle.

Straight out. NOW!

He pushed me, Sir.

NOW! Mop it up quick; then see me at the end and stay behind five minutes.

What, Sir? He doesn't deserve a detention for that. Wasn't his fault the bottle slipped.
Yes, Sir, that's unfair.
I'm wounded by that, Sir, really am.

Wounded? By water?

Naw, by your comments. Didn't believe me, did you?
He's a very sensitive boy, Sir.

Join him at the end for YOUR detention. Three minutes left to complete 9C.
Yes, now what? YOU with your hand half raised.

Nuffin' Sir, just scratching me head.

A QUIET TWO MINUTES INTERRUPTED ONLY BY
SOMEONE SAYING "SHARK".

OK, let's swop your work over to mark it. What's the answer to the first question? You over there.

Urgh?

I told you, you'd be first. Do you have an answer?

No Response.

What's this squiggle? Very nice. A drawing of an oak tree. Join these two lads over there and see me at the end. Yes, over by the window...

Did it hurt, Sir?

Did what hurt?

Having that tattoo, Sir?

What tattoo?

On your neck, Sir. At the side just above your collar.

I've no tattoo!!

Must be dirt.
He was in a rush this morning. [FROM BACK OF ROOM]

OK, cut that out now... get back to the factor trees. What, now?

My answers are TWO, TWO, TWO, THREE, and THREE for 72, Sir.

Oh. Oh… good. Yes. Top fellow. Spot on!

Now the second question. The number 75. What prime numbers do you have at the end of the branches of your factor tree, Wesley?

I've made five, 'cause it ends in a five. Then…
Sir, my pencil's broke.

Broken? Borrow one from a friend.

He doesn't have any friends, Sir.

MUTED LAUGHTER.

Don't get up. You, yes, YOU! Lend him a sharpener. Quick!

Quickly, Sir.

Lend him your sharpener, quickly. NOW!

He won't give it back, Sir. I know him. He's mean.

Yes he will. Don't… DON'T throw. Carry on Wesley.

I've got a FIVE, a SIX, and a TWO to make 60.

That's OK so far. What's he missed? What? Stop hitting over there.

He called my sister fat, Sir. Are you going to let him get away with that?

Both of you. Not really sensible, eh? Grow up… and see me at…

But Huang's right. Freddie's sister is fat, Sir. He was only telling the truth.

See me at the end. You two… and you.

Getting a detention for telling the truth. That's harsh, Sir.
Would you rather he lied, Sir?

OK, the answers to the first six questions are on the board now. Put your hands up if you got at least four correct.

Haven't started yet. What with all this going on.
Got three, Sir.
What's all that got to do with James Bond, Sir?
Nuffin', he just wanted us to think Maths is interesting.

CHATTERING.

You, join the party at the end. Everyone NOW go to page 57. Questions seven to 12, and that includes… YOU. Since when were you not part of everyone? Not very clever, young fellow. Sit down. Join the rest at the end.

Lucky, Patello. Yuh gets a rest at end.

And… *[PAUSE]* AND for those that like a challenge there are extension questions on page… where's my book; the one that was on my desk?

And the board pen? Where's the board pen?

Must have walked, Sir.
It was getting bored. Your board pen, Sir.

LAUGHTER.

OK, boy on front row, hand back the book. YOU, with the ginger hair. Join the detention group at the end. And stop smiling.

That's racist, Sir. You can't sanction him 'cause he's got red hair.
His's aint red. My sister's is really red. She uses beetle blood.

COLLECTIVE URGHHHHH.

I needed the book, Sir. He was on the next page.

Give it back. Here. Now. Thank you.

SLAP! [BOOK BEING DROPPED DOWN]

You're unfair. Blaming him for trying to get on with his work. Unfair. Isn't he?

Yeahh!!

Thank you. Where's the board pen? Who's seen it, now?

SILENCE – AS IF THE BOYS ARE REALLY CONCENTRATING.

OK. TIME OUT! Two minutes while we find my pen and I'll add two minutes to the end of lesson.

You can't do that, Sir. I've already got a detention with the Vice Principal and I can't be late.
So have I.

MILD CHUCKLES FROM BACK [SOUNDS LIKE VICE PRINCIPAL].

It's under his desk – THERE Sir. Must 'ave rolled.

Thank you. Now let's get back to…

BUMP! SOUNDS OF A STRUGGLE.

Get off! Give mee…

You! What's going on back there? What's your name?

McNally, Sir.

What are you doing out of your seat, boy?

Sir, him over there, he's got my bag…

He's nowhere near you. Sit down. NOW!

I need my bag, Sir. Give it 'ere.
Sir. Harsh to have a go at McNally, Sir. He needs his bag to do the work.

STOP right there! McNally, go and sit down, right now. Go on. Back to your seat. NOW! How did it get there, three rows away?

Don't know, Sir, someone must've taken it and it moved itself back.
Must 'ave rolled, Sir. Like your pen.

YOU! Yes, you. Stop smiling. Bring his bag out to me. NOW! The rest of you get on with your work.

Stay behind at the end. Both of you. You for taking it. You for being out of your seat.

That's unfair, Sir. Wasn't McNally's fault. He didn't take his own bag, did he?

Urgh? THAT'S IT!! No one leaves his desk without permission. No! It's the school rules. Are you going to sit down, please?

But someone else took it. He didn't have anything to do with it.

Do you want to join him at the end? I'll see you as well.

RELATIVE QUIET.
TWO MINUTES.

RING!!!!

As you leave the room I want you to… STAY, lads. Stay! I want you to put your worksheets neatly on this front desk. OK, boys at front, you may go.

Door Creaks Open.

Stay back. You. Don't get up yet. Just the front row. The rest of you remain seated until I tell you to…

General Clamour. Bags on Desks. Chattering.

Good. Now let's have a bit of order.

Stop. STOP! SIT BACK DOWN! What do you two want? I've not asked you to leave, yet.

Bringing out our worksheets, Sir.

More Clamour.

Will you all go back and sit down until released?

Shuffling.

OK, you two are sitting down nicely. You can go.

Door Opening.

Out you go. Not you lot. Stay. STAY!!

More Shuffling [Louder.]

Stop. Everyone stays put until I say.

But you said we could go.

We were the ones sitting down, Sir. Now you are holding US back when they're the trouble.

Unfair, Sir.

DOOR OPENING. RUSHED FOOTSTEPS. CLAMOUR.

Stop. No-one will leave until I say.

NOISE OF SOMEONE BACKING INTO DOOR.

Ouch, my elbow.

Bet that hurts, Sir.
Sir, Sir, here's my work.
And mine.
Here's mine. I got to question number eleven, Sir. Think they're all right. Can you check?
Can I have a Mars Bar?

Will you please stop pushing and shoving? No-one goes through this door 'til there's complete order. Now go back to your seats and SIT until I let you go one by one.

Back! Sit! SIT!

We're not dogs, Sir.

You two can leave now. The rest of you stay seated.

Sir, we've got another lesson. It's five minutes gone, now. We'll be late. We've got Awesome next. He'll not like you holding us back.

ONE MINUTE PASSES, WITH RELATIVE CALM.

OK, orderly fashion now. Front row, first. Two at a time.

GENERAL MUTTERING.

Place your sheets on the table tidily. Not on the floor. What are you doing now?

Why you getting' at me again? I'm only pickin' up all the sheets he's knocked off the desk.

STOP trampling over him. Give him space.

But Sir, we're in a hurry, the bell went ages ago.

RIGHT, leave them there. Everyone go! NOW.

*RUSHING FEET. CROWD NOISES. DOOR SHUTTING
WITH SOME FORCE.
THEN SILENCE.*

Well, Godfrey. What do we make of that?

Not sure, Vice Principal? Sorry, Vice Principal, I didn't have time to tell them where to go next. They may not know where…

Over lunch, Godfrey. Let's discuss it over lunch.

Maybe Vice Principal, they've…

Over lunch… and stop touching your neck, Godfrey, it's just a mark.

Jack, what are you still doing here? You should have left by now. Off you go, boy. Go on. Join the others.

Just listening to the music, Mr Vice Principal, Sir. One of my favourites the Kaiser Chiefs.

Only Jack seems to be around to hear 'Never miss a beat' softly playing in the background.

Special Times, Special Places.

Good, enter in single file, take your places quickly. Good lunch today, gentlemen? Pizza with cheesy chips, and the chocolate roly-poly with ice cream and custard – lovely! You probably needed that after your Mission practice. A less involving lesson now. We still need your full attention, but you'll be able to sit back a bit.

Ready. Let's go! Thank you, gentlemen. Come on you stragglers. Sharpen up! Too much custard, eh? Thank you... I need to tell you who took the prizes last lesson for the best Combos.

SILENCE.

Well. WELL! Prime Numbers. And what a prime performance. The longer break should tell you – you were great. Mr Godfrey asked for 20 answers; there was hardly any time to do three or four. Despite being such a new group, that was brilliant. You're all well on target to get Mission Musketeer medals. As for Mr Godfrey? He's taking an extra break...

CHEERING.

...which, gentlemen, is something he can't do most days in school, what with one class following swiftly on behind another.

Your lesson. We really liked the bag tactic, the way most of you picked up on the laughter Combo and we even spotted a bit of misdirection. Also the Bell Rush was awesome. The way some of you were jumping up at the door. No extra special prizes this time as we were specifically looking at Combos where everyone could be involved. Everyone WAS involved. So EVERYONE gets a prize!

MORE CHEERING.

Yes, you, over there? Speak up, now.

Sir, I know we didn't really get a sanction from Mr Godfrey for messing about with McNally's rucksack, but what should we have done to stop sanctions altogether?

As those of you in his group know, gentlemen, I was observing Mr Godfrey's lesson and saw the incident in which two of you were asked to stay behind at 3.30, so I feel able to comment. Snitch and snatch is a good tactic at any time, at the start of a lesson when people are coming in, or during quiet periods. You chose the latter and were right to do so. However, Mr Godfrey had started to get the class settled and so was less flustered than he had been earlier. Basically, he was ready for you. You did well in the first phase to move the rucksack back at least three rows. Where you could have improved the tactic was in the second and third phases when backing him up. McNally got up for his rucksack and started to push and pull the other boy. But then only one person joined in.

For a full snitch Combo, at least eight could have backed up McNally by arguing that justice isn't being done, to remind your teacher that Mrs Awesome would never be so unfair, or how parents might need to be brought in if the rucksack had been damaged. Together with those who moved the rucksack back, nearly half the class might have been involved. Faced with such numbers and an edict from the Head not to give whole class detentions, a teacher needs to be on top form to decide what to do next. Really sharp. Most are too worn out to bother; they just buckle under and do little or nothing.

Also at this early stage might be an opportunity to discuss how the rucksack got there. The boy who ended up with McNally's bag should have professed his innocence. "Sir, how could I get that from over there?" Also "someone must have thrown it" is an effective misdirection. This can lead to others chipping in with their thoughts on who had thrown it, even though you all know that no-one threw anything – it was a pass-back tactic. By now the teacher is completely off-task and starting to wonder what really had happened. If he does give a sanction, then some of you should have picked up on the fact that the accused might miss his bus if he stays behind at 3.30 'cause he lives in such and such a place. Others might then correct this pupil by saying "No, he lives much further away than that." Just little ways to divert the conversation away from the original misdemeanour. By the end the teacher will be more bothered with the times of buses and whether parents are likely to complain and, particularly if McNally has sat down again and isn't involved in this secondary argument, will almost have forgotten about the bag. The original incident followed by your unprovoked debate, with everyone trying to help the teacher with bus facts, could have taken up another four or five minutes. At most, the teacher might get someone to stay behind at lunchtime, but major sanctions are rare.

Having said all of that, it was great to see you try such a tactic to break up the engagement. Who was it that passed the rucksack back in the first place? Well done, lad. Also McNally and the two who said it was unfair. Great move. Yes, question from over there?

Been puzzling us all night, Sir. Why do you call it the Snitch and Snatch and not the other way round?

Yes, Sir, you snatch first then someone snitches.

Hmmm. It's always been so, I guess. Must sound better or something. Like snakes and ladders, fish and chips, tea and cake. Doesn't really matter. Anyway, you all showed us that you are close to mastering it. Well done, gentlemen.

SLIGHT PAUSE.

Let's press on. Sometimes school buildings, school systems and the school day just provide us with times and places that actually help the Mission. Bonus opportunities, courtesy the education system! Relax now as we describe some special school places. Where to start? Where better than YOUR classroom? Then, for a bit of fun, we'll conclude this lesson with some less familiar places – rooms of mystery that you might just like to learn about. But let's start with your classroom.

I said **your classroom** but more accurately I should have said Mrs White's classroom and Mr Black's classroom, because teachers nowadays usually think that the classroom they've been assigned to is theirs. How wrong can they be? This teacher misconception is understandable; they teach most lessons in the same classroom, they are encouraged to assume ownership, they hold the key to the door. But in the classroom you are in the majority, you are the ones in control.

As you'll learn tomorrow, today's classroom arrangements

seem to have been designed to help the Mission. It wasn't always so, but more about the good, old ways when we get to that lesson.

We've mentioned odd tactics with classroom windows and blinds. Then there are other features like the posters, the furniture, the general decor. Here's the stressor. Once a teacher takes ownership of his or her room, then they feel responsible for the way it looks and get more and more stressed when boys alter things.

The Head helps here. Many a Head will warn classroom teachers that their rooms must be pristine at all times, as the school never knows who might make a surprise visit. Prospective new parents, a school governor maybe, the local Education Authority schools' officer, the Education Secretary – anyone might turn up and at any time. The Head will tell the teacher what he'd like to see, such as nice new posters showing the latest work of some enthusiastic class, and what he'd not like to see: torn posters, graffiti on walls and desks, gum underneath desks, litter. So long as everything is in order, the Head's happy. Now I'm not suggesting you go mad and trash the room. Far from it. That would bring in the senior staff. And we all have to live in the place. But little things that are not quite right, little things that only your classroom teachers will notice, will get them doubting their own abilities to run their room. When this happens, when control breaks down, then stress breaks out. Let's note down two or three simple classroom tactics.

Tactic Thirty-Five – Be computer literate.

If there's one classroom feature that has teachers automatically doubting their abilities, it's their classroom computer. Most

197

teachers are computer literate. But NOT that computer literate. They have little time to learn all those new apps, whereas boys do… under the desk during French, or whenever.

Every school has a slightly different IT system – as different as the technicians that commission them. School IT technicians just can't stop downloading *things*. Anything new and they just have to try it out. They have all the time in the world to experiment. New systems, new programmes. They seem to find them exciting; the overworked teacher just finds them confusing. On top of that, computers have a natural tendency to glitches. Doubt doesn't just creep in; it comes in a digital rush.

They're good.

Huh?

Digital Rush, the band, Sir.

OK. If you say so. I'll continue.

Teachers have little faith in their ability with computers. They are only too pleased for some help; and teachers think that every child nowadays is a born computer whiz. So whenever the screen goes blank, or everything's off-centre, you can offer to press a few keys. Again you'll seem to be helpful when really you're just experimenting. Fun, though, and the delays it will cause will just add to the teacher's frustration.

Now, that's with the teacher's permission to meddle. In full view. Just think what you can come up with when his back is turned. Why not introduce a Manchester United screen saver, add some obscure games website to his favourites list, or just make the writing on the interactive whiteboard appear upside down in orange?

Tactic Thirty-Six – Get interactive with the whiteboard.

The whiteboards, gentlemen. Two types here, the ordinary plastic one and the interactive one. You might be helpful by offering to clean the plastic whiteboard at the start or end of the day. Removing pen marks is never straightforward, just as likely to leave a smudgy mess that can turn a whiteboard grey, along with your teacher's hair.

The interactive whiteboard is a different matter. It has wires. Wires pull out just when the teacher isn't expecting it. The projector rarely casts the teacher's lesson full square on the screen. So any nudge of wires or projector as you enter the room *en masse* will probably go unnoticed, but will leave the teacher cursing the equipment in the room. And if it happens nearly every day, then the stress will just magnify.

Tactic Thirty-Seven – Take close notice.

Then, in the typical classroom there's the notice board. The Head will insist that teachers fill any blank spaces with examples of your work, or with posters about attainment levels in their subject and keywords. Keywords, like *gerund* and *past participle*. How daft is that? Talking to your mates you don't stop every 10 seconds to think "is that a gerund", or "I'm using the passive, ablative".

But schools think that these words stuck up on the walls *in your face* every day may somehow sink in and help you to write better, speak proper like and so on. Ridiculous, innit?

Notice boards, gentlemen, provide you with a great stress opportunity. Nearly half the notice boards you'll come across are just painted bits of hardboard, some just walls, some card stuck over asbestos. To spruce them up, teachers are provided with rolls and rolls of wavy strips. Different colours. They staple these around the edge of the area they expect to use as their notice board. Note, I said "staple". They are never glued on, 'cos next term they'll need to replace them with next term's work.

If you push your finger inside the strip, the wavy paper will split and come away from the wall – and one end will dangle down. An alert teacher will staple this back immediately after the lesson. But if she doesn't, that strip is there for the next class to pull at. It all adds up to more work for the teacher, more stress and then she begins to question why she didn't see who had torn it.

If you sit next to the wall, then best not to pull at these strips – you'll be a suspect. Some teachers tend to place the better-behaved pupils next to the walls, but that doesn't stop you taking a tug as you are walking past, and you may get a wall-side nerd into trouble.

At the end of the day, many a teacher will look round their room and wonder why posters curl off the walls, why the computer stops talking to the interactive whiteboard, why the floor is covered in sweet wrappers when they didn't see anyone eating.

Finally, things can magically appear in classrooms, particularly on the ceilings (the work of spitball wizards), under desks and the odd comment might scribble itself across a desk or wall, like

"Mr B smells of acetone disulphide". These will get him doubting himself, if not his knowledge of organic chemistry.

Room tactics don't start and end in the classroom; let's move on now to places outside the classroom. *Movement* is the operative word. We'll start with the corridors, then look inside rooms normally reserved for adults only.

TACTIC THIRTY-EIGHT – CORRIDORS OF POWER.

Teachers can never really unwind while pupils are around. Full-on concentration 100% of their time in class. But they may take the odd breather, especially at break-time when walking to the Staffroom. Don't let them. As you walk past, ask them a question. "Have you seen John, Sir?" or "when did you say the coursework was due?" Anything to break up their quiet moment. Year 7s are good at this. Gullible NEWTs actually appreciate such attention; they think they must be popular. But really we're taking a few moments out of their relaxation time.

You can delay starting your next lesson by walking the wrong way down corridors as some smart teacher is sure to send you back the other way; a good ruse here is to walk a few metres past your classroom door and start to walk back as if you are coming the wrong way. In turning you back to walk in the correct direction, an officious teacher may send you on a round-trip that delays your entrance by several minutes; another opportunity to arrive late with an excuse.

To or from the Sports Hall, the Food Technology kitchens, the science labs – why not walk a little slower than usual and thereby delay the start of the next lesson. Then there's one school

building, one regular activity that provides the ultimate SloPro
Combo. Tactic 39 – it's a beauty!

Tactic Thirty-Nine – Assemblies, disassemble them.
(The ultimate Cross-year SloPro Combo.)

OK, gentlemen, every time you and your group slow down the
start of a lesson, it helps the whole class. But there's one place
where you'll not only be helping yourselves, but every other pupil
in the school – The Assembly Hall. Assemblies usually take place
at the start or end of the day when schools need everyone to be
together – all the teachers and all the pupils – all at the same time.
They usually take place in the Main Hall. Bit like at your primary
school, but a much bigger hall, and ten times more pupils.

Full school assemblies are considered to be very important.
Especially by the Deputy Head, as this is his big opportunity.
Sure it's an opportunity to give you the odd bit of school news,
which may or may not be important, to pass on something he
thinks you need to think about, to pass out Merit badges. All of
these things. But more importantly to the Deputy Head, a whole
school assembly provides an opportunity for him to impress
his fellow leadership team. The more vague and philosophical
the talk, the better. He needs to be seen to be well read in some
subject particularly one that the Head is interested in. It's all very
necessary if he's to progress through the ranks.

In many schools, before going to assemblies, pupils meet in
Form Groups to be registered, then walk calmly to the hall, line
up ready to sit in prearranged places. Sit gracefully. And then
quietly listen. Imagine it, hundreds of boys sitting in orderly

silence, save the odd cough, teachers stood at the sides of their groups, watching closely. All in awe of the occasion, all in awe of the speaker. Hanging on to the Deputy Head's every word. Don't worry. Doesn't happen.

After registration in your classroom, your form teacher will direct you to the assembly. Remember to walk there slowly; after all you've been told again and again not to rush around the place. Perhaps the odd boy can forget the way to the hall or go walkabout. Or go back to his classroom for something he's left behind. Lost boys mean lost time.

Alternatively, as pupils leave the form teacher's classroom, one or two boffins could approach the teacher to ask some relevant question about that day's notices. This is to make sure the teacher is delayed and separated from the form group she is policing. She'll then need to lock up her room and hurry to catch up with her class. If she gets to the hall after them, then she'll have less time to count them all to make sure they're all there.

And don't *forget to forget* that you've been told *not to forget* to leave your schoolbags behind in your form room. Just take everything along as you might to any class. Outside the hall, what do 1000 boys do with 1000 school bags? Take them back to their classrooms? Takes too long. No, leave them in the doorway to the hall. The pile of bags forms a barrier for everyone to jump over, kick out at or – with a carefully-aimed push – a nerd tripper upper. Chaos.

Whatever. Lining up to enter and checking into your seats takes time. So take your time! Think about it. To fill a 300-seat aircraft needs a check-in and embarkation time of about two hours. How can anyone expect teachers to fill a hall with hundreds of pupils in just a few minutes?

Also on your way to assembly why not loosen your tie, pull out your shirt, leave your jacket behind, forget to change from your trainers. Any watching teacher can't ignore it. They will NEED to pull you up as they're also being watched by fellow teachers including the Head. They will need to demonstrate always that they are putting school policy into action. So they'll stop you to get you to tidy up. Great. That introduces delay. When asked to do this or that, stop walking and adjust your uniform accordingly. Say, "Sorry, Sir" as if it's unintentional. Only takes a moment, but it's a moment that holds up everyone behind you in the queue for the hall. The more boys that make adjustments, the longer it will take for everyone to enter and sit down. Then once inside loosen your tie again, lean back on your chair, tip over to annoy those in the row behind or extend your legs to upset the row in front. Sweet! Anything to get a response from those around you that will attract a teacher's attention and take up a few more seconds.

In most schools the hall is used throughout the day, so the chairs in assembly need to be set out by a most caring caretaker before school. Certain classes will sit in certain rows, such as Year 7s at the front, Year 9s in rows eight to ten and so on. But boys come to assembly from all parts of the school in dribs and drabs. They usually enter in no particular order, classes within the same year at different times, and Year 7s are rarely the first classes to arrive. So if someone was to miscount the rows and sit down in the wrong place, he might just set a trend. The rest of his class might just follow him, all sitting down in the wrong rows. When the correct year group arrives, a mad dance of boys pushing and shoving their way to the correct rows can ensue. Takes some sorting out.

Once assembly is underway, look out for opportunities to make a whole-school noise. An odd remark from the speaker might just generate a cheer or a whooooo.

Yes, quite. Such delays to the assembly will cascade down throughout the school day. The first lesson after assembly is always late to start. The poor teachers giving those lessons just find themselves under extra pressure to fit in their planned topics.

Any tactic that involves boys from different years working together is really confusing to teachers. Assemblies provide the most effective, ultimate cross-year, SloPro opportunity; when you appear to have dropped your standards of behaviour or dress, teachers are required to remind you what you should or shouldn't be doing. It all takes time. Good aren't they, these school rules!

The assembly hall and the classroom are good places to try out tactics. Now sit back while we visit a few *rooms-of-mystery* found in every school, some rivalling the most harrowing haunts of Hogwarts.

The Secretarial Suite.

This is a place you need to get to know. It's staffed by nice sympathetic people, not teachers. Some schools allow older pupils to get some work experience by doing odd jobs for the office, like filling envelopes and photocopying. If the office experience opportunity arises then take it; a few misdirected letters to parents can cause havoc. Try to wangle your way into answering the phones. It's fun. And it can be disconcerting to any teacher when he phones the office from his classroom to find out why you are not in class, to hear your voice on the other end of the phone.

The Caretaker's Office.

In most schools, this place is no bigger than a broom cupboard and is full of... brooms... and mops and brushes. A small, battered desk sits under the dirt-encrusted window (all the other windows in the school are spotless as the caretaker has washed them). And on that desk, a cracked cup, always half-full, and next to the cup the biggest bunch of keys you've ever seen and a plastic bag full of pens he's picked out of the bushes. You shouldn't ever need to enter this room. The only mystery about this place is why on his battered desk there is *always* a tin tray with six or seven odd sized, rusty screws.

The Head's Office.

Every school is a mass of activity, swarms of people, hustle and bustle, especially at break-time. You can't get away from the crowd. Everywhere you'll see teachers bumping into each other by accident, boys bumping into boys on purpose, teachers shimmying around pupils, boys crashing through doors. It's bedlam. But there's one exception. The Head's office.

For most of the time it's a place of calm and quiet. That's because only he is allowed in there, by himself. What does he do there? No-one knows. Even the Assistant Heads only occasionally get invited in.

In summary, it's the ultimate place of mystery. You don't ever want to go there. But if you hear that a teacher has been called there, then it's a good sign that your mission tactics are working. Either the teacher will have been called there to be told off or he's about to crack and is seeking advice from the Head on how to relieve the stress.

The Staffroom

Finally, there's one room few pupils are allowed inside. And for very good reasons. The Staffroom. Of course you may sometimes be asked to take something to your teacher in the Staffroom. Be prepared for a long wait – no-one knows why, but you'll find it's always something that keeps you hanging around outside for most of your break.

While you are waiting you may get to glance through that small window in the Staffroom door. It's always a small window. And you'll hardly see anything as the main activity is usually through a second set of double-doors or around a corner out of sight.

Few tips now on how to cut down the waiting. Imagine it's break-time. You've been called to the Staffroom. Don't go straight away, leave it for at least eight minutes. This is because teachers are far too busy to come out to see you during the first five minutes; they're busy rucking and mauling their way to a quick caffeine fix.

Every Staffroom has a sink, usually on the left just as you come into the room. The sink is set into a worktop and adjacent to a hot-water dispenser, dripping into a plastic tray. The drips are scalding, but teachers develop asbestos hands. Next there's a cold-water dispenser (ever wondered why teachers never buy bottled water).

On the main worktop there are three ever-presents. A bowl of teabags, a plate of cakes and a plastic microwave dinner tray containing something gooey. Where they come from no-one is quite sure, but they are there every break.

Imagine the scene one minute before the break. Two teachers will get there early, the same two most days. Don't they have classes to teach? Then the rush! Dozens of teachers swarm into the place. It's always a scramble to grab a favourite cup. Some teachers have perfected the on-the-run, bag-to-cup manoeuvre – a rapid single movement grab and scoop action. Few have mastered the art of taking a cake at speed. The first ones to the cakes just stand there looking and prodding, as though they've never seen a cake before.

Some pause for a slightly defensive "should I take one or two?" This creates the first bottleneck. Rampant teachers, 30 or 40 of them, pushing and shoving into each other, mouths frothing with cake.

Now I don't know why, but there are always two or three teachers stood right in front of the hot water dispenser, chatting about something and nothing. Every break, every day, they're guaranteed to be there. The Blockers. They don't seem to see the other thirty teachers trying to top up their cups. The more nimble teachers manoeuvre around the Blockers like experts at a barn dance, filling their cups, spooning their teabags, then with the skill of a spin bowler, they toss the tea bag in a curving action around the Blockers into an open plastic compost bin.

Yes, compost bin. You might expect a flip-top kitchen bin near a sink, but flip-tops are rarely seen outside the Food Tech Department. Compost bins. Schools must get them on an environmental grant or something, the outcome of an application by some new geography teacher with the noble intention, yet never the time, to start a recycling club. Anyway these black plastic composters usually end up in the Staffroom sans tops yet complete with daily bin liners.

Anyway, you boys waiting outside the room are the last things on teachers' minds during those first five minutes. So leave it until eight to ten minutes in. By this time teachers will be relaxing with their mugs and cake. Knock loudly on the door and say to the first NEWT to answer "Mrs Jones has requested me to come here. Can you ask her if she's available, please?" Even if you aren't in trouble, maybe helping to carry something to the room, you should always look tidy and as though you have come to be reprimanded, as this then gives the NEWT extra impetus to find Mrs Jones. Yes, you have a question.

Good question, but during break-time the more experienced teachers just don't respond to a knock on the door. NEWTs are keen… and have standards.

You know how teachers are always telling you to tuck in your shirt, tighten your tie, wash the ink off your hands. That kind of thing. They seem to be paragons of neatness and tidiness. Nothing could be further from reality. Go into any Staffroom in the country and you'll find crumbs on the seats, papers strewn all over the place, old copies of magazines cluttering the tables (usually with tea-stains on the cover in some loose Olympic ring formation). On every table there's an unwashed mug with week-old coffee deposits, half an inch thick. Disgusting! And at the side, usually near the photocopier, there are piles of photocopied sheets and a curled, yellow *"every-teacher-take-one"* post-it note that's somehow drifted onto the floor nearby.

Staffrooms are a shambles. The only exception is the first week of term after some kind NEWT has spent their holidays hoovering and organising, oh… and during Ofsted weeks when everybody's tidying.

Chaotic! You wouldn't believe the way teachers act. That Staffroom sink; it's piled high with dirty cups, plates and broken plastic forks. Messy!

Let's give them one thing; teachers have a really good sense of irony. Above the sink – in every school – there are laminated signs saying **Clean It Up**, or **This Dishwasher actually takes Teachers' Cups** or **Don't leave pots on the draining board**. No one ever takes any notice of these except perhaps the NEWTs and the exasperated person who pins them so neatly above the sink.

That's another Staffroom mystery. Who puts these signs up?

As I said, they're in every school. The chief suspect is always an English teacher (they are the only ones who know where to put the apostrophes) and she's usually called Janet or Jane or some such name. But that's pure speculation, no-one ever owns up to such signage.

Most teachers hardly ever wash their cups (the Unions or someone won't allow them). In fact some schools appoint one of the office or canteen staff to actually do the pot-washing. How lazy can you get?

Even teachers that do put cups in the dishwasher rarely check to see if the cups inside are dirty or ready to be taken out. It all ends up with the very clean ones being washed again and again, three or four times before they are retrieved. It's a complete waste of energy and water, talk about teachers being environmentally green. All that's green is the mould on the draining board.

But enough about this mess. There's another thing you'll notice about Staffrooms – one or two teachers quietly sitting by themselves on opposite sides of the room. Supplies. And at least three others are slouching back in their chairs at exactly 45 degrees, just looking into space. Two of these are NEWTs wondering perhaps what they've got themselves into by becoming teachers; the third is an older teacher taking a nap. Some days they just gaze at the posters.

Posters. Did we say "posters"? Not just above the sink, but everywhere, even the pillars and the ceiling beams are full of posters. So many posters that no-one has time to read them all, but more about why they are important later.

Now on the opposite side of the room to the sink is a suite of four computers complete with chairs that always seem, well, unstable – the chairs that is, the stability of the teachers is not in question. At two of the computers there are teachers, not typing, but chatting – always merrily – the other two computers are unattended but each will have something half-prepared on the screen, have a jacket over the back of the chair and a pencil case strategically placed across the keyboard. You can bet these HOGS are student teachers. At some times of the year the place is full of them snuffling around the Staffroom, cluttering the seats with their ever-optimistic, half-written theses on the finer arts of teaching.

At the side, there's the telephone. Placed in the noisiest part of the room, beleaguered by cross talk. It's there mainly for teachers to phone your parents, potentially another kind of cross talk, but as your parents are out at work when teachers are in, the result is usually a frustrating, watered down answerphone message.

Let's just return to those wall posters and why Mission Musketeers might need to take them seriously. Many of these posters are about YOU! Now there are the helpful ones that tell everyone when the exams are and which pupils are involved. Dates of parents' evenings, school concerts and days out. Useful.

Then there are the motivational ones. They suggest to teachers that many of them need motivating to carry on. A clear sign that our Mission tactics are working. Inadvertently spreading the Mission's message.

Around the end of August. It happens in every school. Deputy Heads struggle in with armfuls of these inspirational posters, pockets full of blue tack, furtively – making sure that the hoovering NEWT isn't in that day – and they plaster the walls with signs. This signing is, many would say, one of the main duties of a Deputy Head, particularly as they only teach a handful of classes each week. Examples of pupil-related posters might be:

- Catch them being good!
- They're not his pupils or her pupils, they are OUR pupils.
- Stop flocking?????????
- Every expert was once a beginner.
- Consistency makes a school a team.
- Touch a heart – Open a mind.
- Accolades, not criticism.
- School rules = classroom rules
- Learning should lead to fun. And fun should lead to learning.
- Fair isn't the same as everyone getting the same.

Oh, and somewhere near the Union board, in quite large letters

FAIR PAY FOR TEACHERS AND
STOP THEM ROBBING OUR PENSIONS.

So that's a bit about school rooms, gentlemen. Take a five-minute breather while we get ready for the Plenary.

PLENARY.

I know from some of the comments at break-time that you have quite a few questions about teachers themselves and why they put up with the stresses of school life, so we'll take this opportunity to say a bit more about teachers and take your specific questions.

You may have got the idea that our Mission seems to be directed against teachers as individuals. As we said earlier this week, gentlemen, we don't really want you to think that. The Mission is nothing personal. It's really not the classroom teacher's fault. The real oppressive power comes from the top. The education system. And some outside influences that we'll tell you about tomorrow.

Nowadays, your ordinary teachers, particularly when they are starting out, don't have much control over school rules and the underlying aims of the curriculum. It's just a bit unfortunate that they are the frontline troops. We've done them down a bit over the week and maybe on this penultimate day it's now time to give their image a boost. After all it wouldn't be much of a Mission challenge if your teachers didn't seem worthy opponents.

Purely with that in mind, who better to do this than the Assistant Deputy Vice Principal? Just for 10 minutes, he's going to put the argument that teachers are really quite outstanding individuals. Listen closely. It's probably the only time in the next few years you'll hear that.

No need to concentrate too hard on his argument. Been a long day. Just sit back and relax.

CLATTERING OF SEATS
BUMP.

Teachers are Outstanding!
InconTEStable, Utterly, Utterly Conclusive Proof.

Good to go, boys! COME ON! I know, you might be surprised to hear what the Vice Principal has just told you, but I'm here to tell you – to prove to you – that most teachers are outstanding. I repeat: OUTSTANDING!! Apart from a few NEWTs and the odd SAG, let's give a big cheer for all teachers. They're outstanding.

HESITANT CHEERING, PETERING OUT.

OK, boys, I was only having you on. Don't get carried away. While most of the stuff that teachers teach isn't worth spending time on, hence the Mission, we need to differentiate between the teacher and the topic. Most teachers are keen... and wholehearted. Don't frown, boys. I'm not just saying that. No, No, really. I've absolutely conclusive proof.

Most teachers are E-N-T-H-U-si-astic! Categorically so. Enthusiastic! And creative! And committed! And very-this and very-that and outstanding in every way. How can I be so sure? It's right out there, in front of our very eyes, every week, there for all to see.

Still not convinced? Just read the JOBS sections of your local paper and the teachers' very own paper, the TES. No matter the school, no matter the subject, nearly every job ad for a classroom teacher asks for "an enthusiastic teacher". And as Heads and Governors always stick carefully by their principles, then they wouldn't employ anyone who wasn't enthusiastic, would they? Simple logic, eh?

There's more! In most schools, teachers also seem to need to be inspiring because they will be joining inspirational and creative departments. These departments are almost always supportive. And innovative. And dynamic!

How long can anything so dynamic stay that way? *[COMMENTS FROM SIDE OF ROOM]*

Thank you, Godfrey, don't butt in. OK, ADVP, please continue to tell the boys why teachers are so outstanding.

Hey, squabble ye not. Listen up, boys. These job ads. It's not just the departments that the ads say are good. In a high percentage of cases, the whole school will be described as outstanding. To emphasise the fact, in most ads the word *Outstanding* is spelled with a capital O. Applicants to teach English grammar usually apply with clenched teeth. And as schools almost always follow the same guidelines when composing the ads, they hardly demonstrate any of the real creativity or innovative thinking they purport to seek.

Hey ho! Teacher recruitment ads say no more than a line or two about the position they wish to fill; a lot more about the department and the school itself. You see these ads aren't primarily aimed at the teachers looking for jobs. Most Heads, always out to spot an opportunity, will see a wider opening. No, these ads are mainly written to impress Ofsted and the authorities, to demonstrate that the Head and governors of the school have read and are committed to the Ofsted guidelines. Or if the ad is in a local paper, to promote the school to prospective parents, the local authorities, and the envious Heads of nearby schools that haven't quite yet become Outstanding.

When it comes to the Ofsted guidelines, this is called being prepared, all part of a school's SEF groundwork.

SEF, Sir?

Something that used to worry Heads. Another thing that's changing. Nothing really for boys to worry about. If you're that interested, Google it.

Job ads, what? If they had any sense, teachers would stash away the ad for the job they eventually took and show it to the Headmaster two or three years later. "Of course I need a pay rise, you appointed an ambitious, enthusiastic, dedicated practitioner". Of course! Of course, teachers know what the reply will be; so they rarely adopt this tactic.

Sure it wouldn't be very encouraging to teachers if the job ads said "we'll make do with absolutely anyone who knows a bit about history or science" or "we're desperate for someone who can do long division".

All job applicants, whatever their profession, like to be sold to. So a bit of enthusiasm is always welcome. But need teaching ads be so longwinded and self-serving? On the board, here's an ad with everything the applicant needs to know.

"Required September. Experienced Teacher or NQT for French. Wandsworth. Apply by 1 May. Further details – see our website."

Now on the board are typical ads. Hundreds of words; you might need to squint a bit. Really cramped fonts, all crammed in.

TAPPING ON INTERACTIVE BOARD.

Look here. Like most things in teaching, these ads follow a certain pattern. See, this hardly demonstrates creativity.

TAP!

216

What do you think this is for?

And this… I could discuss these ads for hours, however just one final point – a lot of schools need to say in these ads that they are committed to child safety and to making a positive contribution to the education of children. Doh? Occasionally they say the teacher should hold children in the highest esteem. Double doh!

Might save some schools a bit of advertising money if they kept their ads short and to the point. You don't get supermarkets taking 150 words to describe a cauliflower.

QUIET CONTEMPLATION, A FEW COUGHS AND MUTTERS.

Count the superlatives.

MORE TAPPING.

So there you have it. Hah, ad break over. I'm good for going.

Thank you, thank you, ADVP. A thoroughly convincing argument that teachers ARE outstanding individuals. A challenge for all our Mission Musketeers. Any questions – on anything we've discussed today?

ODD MURMUR, A BUMP, FOOTSTEPS RECEDING TO BACK OF CLASS.

Questions, please. The gentleman in the polkadot shirt, third row. Are you a *Tour* cyclist?

Not really, Sir... Sir, how will we know if the Mission is working?

When the Mission is working. Be positive, boy.

Sir, WHEN will we know if the Mission is working?

We'll go into all that tomorrow. Won't say any more now. But let me assure you that there are clear signs all around you, gentlemen, that our Mission is successful. Yes, you…

Sir, why DO teachers put up with teaching, WHEN the Mission is working?

Again, tomorrow gentlemen, we'll show you that a lot don't. Remember, we recognise that some teachers will be hard to shift – the Engagers and the Awesomes, and those that have stuck it for years. The Mission is actually very successful when aimed at NEWTs; and our objective is to get them to give up before they've really started. A lot of teachers give up within a few years.

As for those that find it tough, yet stick with it, just human nature, I guess. We all like to pass on what we've learnt ourselves. Can't help it. Even you boys; when didn't you get a thrill about showing someone something you are interested in, like how to download the latest app or to get past level 12 on a new game, or demonstrate some sporting skill you've just mastered? It's not really showing off; just gives you a feeling of being of value to your mates. Teachers are the same. They've learnt something and they just need to pass it on. The problem is the stuff they choose to teach – their specialist subjects – are only special to them; quite irrelevant to most 11 year olds.

But why do they start teaching in the first place, Sir?

Myths and deceptions, teacher misconceptions, that's what. Teachers have somehow got the idea that teaching is a worthwhile career – a vocation, or some such concept. The job stability, the pay and the holidays may also draw them in; *benefits* they soon realise are not what they first seemed. Look, when it comes to a teachers' hourly pay, pensions and holidays, there are many sleights of hand. On reading their first job description, gullible NEWTs, will note that they are contracted to work 1265 directed hours a year, over 40 or so weeks, leaving about 12 weeks for a holiday or three. Divide those 1265 hours by 40 and you'll see it's not bad. Only about 31 hours a week. Or six hours a day. With at least three of those hours every week free for planning and preparing lessons. Pretty good, eh?

Mr and Ms Trusting Teacher sign these contracts with glee. But the devil is in the detail. They failed to spot the word *directed* when describing the hours. These hours are as near to real time as something you'd see in Dr Who. Anyone planning 20 one-hour lessons a week can't possibly plan all 20 in just three hours. Only politicians are inexperienced enough to think it's possible. Moreover, NEWTs like to over-plan their lessons; the creative juices start to flow. They get carried away producing *Blue Peter* resources out of cardboard.

In these job contracts there's not much detail about the time needed to mark homeworks, to police detentions, to design and arrange wall posters. The average conscientious teacher does 55 to 60 hours per week. That's 12 hours a day. Plus travel time to work.

New appointment contracts are laden with what seem to be false promises, lies and deceptions. The funny thing is that half the time it's not the school (they play by the legal rules) but the teachers deceiving themselves on how much time they've got. Curiously some teachers enjoy every minute planning their lessons, designing new teaching resources – not realising that they are over-doing it, nor that the best laid plans, no matter how creative the resources, sometimes come unstuck during a lesson.

You saw Mr Godfrey's heavy day on Tuesday. Bet you he didn't think it would be such when he first decided to go into teaching. He signed up and like most new teachers got consumed by it all.

And on that cautionary note, gentlemen, it's time to end today's Summer Skool. This afternoon we looked inside schools to learn how some of the rooms help the Mission. Tomorrow we'll be looking outside your school – to consider some unlikely help for the Mission and we'll teach you a bit of *formative assessment*, ways to look out for signs that the Mission is really effective.

Let's leave Summer Skool carefully now. In ones and twos, and watch you're not spotted. Just one more day, then you'll be ready. Ready for the Mission. Ready for the next stage of the revolution.

The boys join in with a thumping rendition of the chorus from T-Rex's 'Children of the Revolution'. As the door clangs shut, singing can still be heard across the playground.

Whispered.
I've decided, Godfrey. That's it. The Major General was right to raise it. Can't let it continue like this. Has to be. No, I won't say 'No'. My decision is final. Tomorrow, we'll have to bring in *The Terminator*.

Day Five

The boys learn that they have outside help. The authorities get involved. A spooky noise upsets the boys. Termination – the inevitable, inescapable finale.

The Mission – You are not Alone.

SHUFFLING AND SEAT NOISES.

Good morning. Final day. Everyone ready. Special day. Special lessons. Special favourites for lunch. And something really exciting for you this afternoon. Something to engage you – hands on and noisy! You'll love it. The highlight many boys tell us. The Grand Summer Skool Finale.

VERY QUIET.

GOOD MORNING, GENTLEMEN!!

Good morning, Mr Vice Principal, Sir. [UNENTHUSIASTIC]

Well, it's the final day of Summer Skool and next term you'll be going forth on your own to practise what we've taught you. Sit up, please. UP! NOW! Are you all excited about the day ahead? You should be.

Or do I detect a certain glumness around the room? You seem a bit zonked out by it all.

Is everyone ready? No, I DO sense a certain quietness around the room? Having incontestably proven to you yesterday that teachers are quite outstanding may not have helped. Hey, it's not unusual. After the excitement of this week, trying out all those tactics, all the hopes, all the anticipation – when it comes to this point on the last day, worries may creep in. It's to be expected, it happens every year at Summer Skool. This final morning, some of you will be a bit unsure of how you are going to get on out there.

Am I right? Bet some of you are thinking "It's OK in theory, but after today it's down to me. What will happen when I get to the secondary school? Will the Mission tactics really work? Will I be the one to slip up and get punished?"

It's natural. It happens to everyone. But, trust me; any such feelings won't last long. Let me assure you, gentlemen, once you get started, you've nothing to fear. As we've said all along, our tactics are rigorously designed to keep you out of major sanctions. No worries. You're young. When you feel ready, that's all; first you could try some of those SloPro tactics that make you look nice and keen.

Look around your new school. Observe the older boys. See how they do it. By the second or third term of Year 7, I promise, you'll be in full swing. Then you can let rip. It'll all fall into place, trust me.

But, gentlemen, it's quite understandable that today the

odd doubt is creeping in. Like base jumping over roofs, reverse grinding over railings, BMX somersaults or diving off the top board at the swimming pool, there'll be nerves at first. But you're boys; you just need to do it.

Perhaps the biggest concern 11 year olds tell us is that you feel, on this the eve of secondary school, that you're on your own. But, think about it, you're not. Every boy in the years above yours will be already out there prosecuting the Mission. Speak to your Year 8s, older boys on the bus, in the playgrounds; soon you'll learn how you too can get involved. Preferred tactics, best targets, where and when. It may take a few weeks, but take my word, it'll come. By this time next year, you'll all be experts.

But better still, you're really, REALLY not alone. There's help. Lots of it. Lots of adults are on our side – including people in real authority, all rallying round to help you with the Mission. Some don't realise that they are helping; but some, we suspect do. These will be powerful allies especially when it comes to applying stress and doubt. Most of these adult allies you'll never meet, and we'll talk about them next lesson. But now we'll look at one or two groups of people nearer to home. People you'll see every day. Mission Allies, if only they knew it.

Your Parents

I know, by your age – 11 or 12 – parents can be a bit over the top. They drive you mad. But they're useful! They can also drive you around. And when it comes to the Mission they are very useful.

Believe it or not parents take a lot of trouble finding you a secondary school. They spend months, sometimes years, searching. Some pay for special tutoring to get you into the best schools, some donate to the school's development fund, some take the Head out to tea.

Put your hands up if you've moved house in the past year. That's parents again; trying to get you a little nearer to a good school. Which conveniently brings me on to our final Summer Skool tactic.

∽

Tactic Forty – Parental controls.

Having chosen your secondary school, parents are desperate to convince themselves that they've made the right decision. They'll ask you questions about the new school almost every night. What did you do in Maths today? Are you learning a foreign language yet? What are your teachers like?

Just shrug and say "It's OK, I suppose". At this early stage don't criticise anything too general, otherwise they'll keep on at you. They might even turn up at the school to check the school dinners are hot. Embarrassing! So just say "Doesn't matter". In time they'll get the message.

But when they ask you about your teachers... well, what an opportunity! But at the start, gentlemen, it's best not to go overboard in your criticism. The casual comment about a teacher and his odd ways of teaching can be far more effective than a full-out attack. Be subtle. Without actually saying so, suggest that things could be better but you don't really want to talk about it. Then sit back and watch what happens.

It'll be obvious to your parents that certain teachers in the school aren't giving you the support you need in your learning. Maybe these teachers don't recognise your undoubted talent, well not the way your parents do. Maybe they don't even recognise you – how could they be so unthinking? Maybe they're singling you out.

Parents will feel that you are only putting up with things because you're young, have no experience of secondary education and don't want to get into trouble at your new school. They'll have to act on your behalf. Phonecalls to the Head of Department, letters to the Head, pointed questions to the teacher on Parents Evening – all great stressors for the poor class teacher. Remember, your comments should only be like occasional sniper fire; you can rely on your parents' imaginations for the full-out rocket attack.

Then huh, huh, there are homeworks. Few boys want to do them. Few teachers want to mark them. But every parent likes to see them, if only to test themselves with what they've forgotten. Funny things homeworks; you are the one that leaves them behind, you haven't the time for them, yet in parents' eyes, if you don't bring homeworks home, it's not really your fault. Magically, it's the school's.

Did I say that your parents already might believe that the school isn't giving you the education and support you deserve? Wherever could they have got such an idea? You'd never believe it. We'll cover that in more detail after the break. But for now, let's consider some more *insiders* that inadvertently pile extra stress on your teachers.

The Head and the SLT

We introduced you to the SLT back on Tuesday – the Senior Leadership Team. All those Heads, Deputies, Assistant Heads. They ARE teachers, they remember what it was like to teach their own classes flat out and they really, genuinely want to support the up-and-coming teachers. But unwittingly they can help the

Mission by placing extra stress and doubt on their underling colleagues.

Let's start with the Head. Basically she's (or he's) a rock, or should I say between a rock... and a hard place. Pressures from above from governors and the authorities; responsibilities for teachers below; squabbles among the secretaries, a cantankerous caretaker with a broken hammer and a sore thumb. What with new initiatives from the government every week and union actions to contend with, the Head can often be forgiven for not knowing which place to start. But Heads must always look in control and must keep up morale, so they have their own office to escape to and, for anything they are not too sure about, they have a book of pat phrases for staff meetings, like "That was a very positive outcome".

Often when trying to help the junior teachers, a Head's efforts can turn into own goals. Any initiative means change. And any change means more things for the over-worked teacher to spend time on. So the Head has to think very carefully when it comes to new proposals.

Sometimes a Head might want to speak to a teacher individually, one-to-one. Imagine you are that teacher. She asks her secretary to email you: "*The Head would like to see you today at 2pm*". That's it. No explanation about why she wants the meeting; to do so might reveal private issues to the secretary. The meeting involves only you; no other member of staff has been summoned. She chooses 2pm as this is your PPA (planning) period; after all she wouldn't want to have to find cover for your lesson. But Heads are busy, sometimes they have unexpected visitors or are called away, and the secretary has to email back to say "*Sorry, the Head would like to put back your meeting until your next free period*" and that's not until Thursday. Now, you are wondering what the original meeting might be about. Has a parent complained? Have you done something wrong? Two or three days to sweat it out.

In such a situation a NEWT's imagination runs riot. By Thursday our NEWT hasn't slept a wink and is totally stressed. And what's the meeting about? Probably the Head, sensitive to the teacher's nervous start, just wants to offer an anxiety management course.

The post of Deputy Head is quite interesting. Most schools have two of them. One to do whatever Deputy Heads do, and the other one's a spare. Usually one is very involved, the other one… well, no-one's sure. Usually quite jovial when dealing with parents and colleagues alike; in assemblies, passing on their experiences of how they did this, how they did that, how you can do things a little better. But their hidden talent is patience. They're your *Heads in Waiting*. They wait and wait. Waiting never seems to bother them; they have it off to a fine art. So much so, that sometimes they will keep the ordinary classroom teachers waiting.

If there are two Deputies in most secondary schools, then statistically half the Deputy Heads will never make it to be *The Head*; their patience turns to despondency, they leave and become educational consultants. Anyway even though they do nothing to stress out NEWTs, Deputy Heads certainly help the Mission. Well not directly. You see NEWTs think that, given their seniority, they must be able to help with any NEWTish problems. But some Deputy Heads have in-trays akin to a bowl of custard; anything dropping into it sinks into oblivion. Three weeks later the teacher, an urgent matter now becoming desperate, is still waiting and the problem is growing.

While Deputy Heads (at least the spare ones) can sometimes seem to be doing nothing, Assistant Heads are the exact opposite. They never stop. Never stop running around, here and there, writing reports and organising change. They are in school to impress, to get on – as a result the classroom teacher just wants to get off. What with all that extra work their actions and initiatives create.

These *not-quite-heads* aren't called the Senior Leadership Team, SLT, for nothing. They're senior; they lead. At the start of term, a few days before you boys go in, that's when the Assistant Heads bring in new theories they've been reading up about all summer. They suggest lots of changes for the year ahead – like new software packages, the latest theories on behaviour, when the school day should start, the times school bells should ring or the optimum length for the dinner hour (shouldn't an hour be 60 minutes?) Lots of new things for both old-timers and NEWTs to take in. NEWTs, impressed by anything the SLTs bring up, are easily taken in. They especially lap up any behaviour tips; they're certain that when they've mastered them then you boys will all fall into line. Old-timers have heard these *really novel* initiatives many times before.

The other teachers called "Head" are the Heads of Departments; they are usually very supportive and loyal to the teachers in their departments so can't directly help the Mission. Except? Except if you are extra good when they are around, they'll think you are well-behaved and give less credence to any complaints about you from their staff.

So generally, SLTs are great for the Mission. SLTs are usually the ones that carry out classroom observations. Constructive comments are all well and good, but their stark reports can often seem like undue criticism to the browbeaten teacher being observed. Teachers HATE observations.

During observations, the observed teacher at the front is concentrating on the topic; the SLT is concentrating on what's going on around the room. From the back she is in a position to see things going on that the teacher can't. So don't disappoint her. During observations, every boy should be taking part in some very minor misdemeanour, nothing too serious, just boys' stuff like pushing your mate, or nicking his pen, gentle fidgeting. Not all at once, mind. Take it in turns. Every few minutes someone should just go off task for a moment or two, long enough for the SLT to note what you are doing. But don't worry. During observations the SLT won't criticise the pupils. She'll blame the teacher for not having eyes in the back of his or her head. Not spotting what half of the class is up to. And as her report may go to the Head for final checking, the more comments she writes, the more he might be impressed with her detail. SLTs are very professional, very hardworking, they generate a lot of paperwork and the more they put in, the more paper that lands on the classroom desk. More reports to read, more information to absorb and more work for the busy classroom teacher.

SLT – Strife for Lowly Teachers.

Going for Growth.

Here's another way a lot of Heads and SLTs inadvertently help the Mission. For the very best and most noble intentions, sometimes pushed by governors and the local authority, they start to believe that the bigger the school the better. You see, when a school gets a good name, Heads can get over-ambitious. The more children they can attract to a school, the more subjects they can afford to offer, the greater their status and the greater the funding for the school.

This helps to explain why a lot of schools aren't satisfied with five days in the working week. They need ten. Something to do with fitting in extra subjects; subjects just to pander to parents –

like philosophy and psychology, Latin and law, classical studies, Mandarin and Serbo-Croat. No pupil takes these subjects, well hardly anyone, but they look good on the school website. Parents like these subjects. Most pupils like softer subjects like Drama and Media studies, Food technology and Animal welfare. It's all fluffy bunnies – in or out of the pot!

So every year the school wants more and more new pupils. Soon the school buildings are crammed to the rafters. In such a scenario, teachers in some departments become extra vulnerable. Maths and English are two such subjects. Unlike many subjects, everyone has to take Maths and English at least to Year 11. There are rarely enough rooms in their dedicated blocks. And this gives our Mission a great opportunity. To fit everyone in, the Head will call on his Deputy Head to juggle the numbers. After weeks of deliberation the Deputy Head will usually come up with one of two solutions. The first is to borrow spare classrooms from other departments like French and History, subjects only a few keen pupils opt for after Year 9, so their departments have lots of empty rooms. The second is to offer the whole curriculum over two weeks with more slots for Maths and English, and Serbo-Croatian studies only on alternate weeks. Now, at least pupils learn English in the English Department (with all those gerunds on the wall). They call these *two-week cycles*.

If your school has two-week cycles or you are required to change classrooms from one week to the next and from one department to another, then rejoice. It's just extra confusion. Teachers have enough trouble remembering what day it is without the order of lessons changing from one week to the next. And when should they set homeworks; is it Tuesday this week or next?

No two rooms have desks in exactly the same place. A change of rooms gives you scope to sit in different places; teachers can't relate your names to where you sit. Also, you can use this for a Combo pretending to fight over desks. "Sir, I normally sit there. Oh, sorry forgot that's on Tuesdays in Room M5." Your group might purposely line up outside the wrong room or even enter and sit down looking ready to start, pretending you're in E3 when you should be in E7. Even without you doing anything, it's a good bet that the box of text books you'll all need for the lesson will be in the wrong room; another solid reason for a 10-minute delay while someone goes to find them. And if your overspill rooms are in a different department, then by now those English textbooks could be anywhere in the school. Better still, if you ever needed an excuse to forget to bring in your homework or just to cause a bit of confusion by bringing your geography books to a Maths lesson then the "Oh, Sir. I forgot it's Week Two" provides the perfect homework get-out clause.

Colleagues.

Further Mission assistance comes from other teachers. Now, 90% of colleagues are nice – but very busy. Too busy. Too involved in their own packed programmes to notice a colleague in difficulties. They may occasionally offer tea, but sympathy...?

And cake, Sir.

OK, and cake. No matter their job, everyone has doubts at some time, particularly when there's a lot of change going on. In schools, change is ALWAYS going on. Teachers in doubt naturally do things to protect their own self-status, but often without thinking it's at the expense of someone who's struggling. In a mad scramble to climb *out of the pond,* someone always needs to be stepped on. NEWTs and TOADS often find themselves in at the deep end.

Awesomes rarely get involved in this; they are too self-secure. Would-be SLTs and student mentors sometimes do, inadvertently, trampling over colleagues as they career-climb, onwards and upwards.

The result is a subtle kind of internal *bullying*. The teachers' unions recognise this, but many ordinary colleagues don't even realise that they're being so judgemental; they're all too busy to analyse how their own actions affect junior colleagues. As far as OUR Mission is concerned, just leave them to get on with it. When he spoke about Combos, the ADVP warned that when it comes to our pupil tactics, we don't like bully-boy stuff. It just lowers the tone of the Mission.

But teachers bullying each other – that's quite a different matter.

Lots of Mission allies, there then, right within the schools. Short chatter-break now. Then, with Mr Godfrey's help, we'll look at some of the Mission-positive ways that the system works when training and recruiting teachers.

CHATTERING.

Hoops and Hurdles.

Now in this lesson, gentlemen, we are going to consider the way your school operates, the common, day-to-day procedures that have been thought out to the finest detail. As we said, the Head and other SLTs will be responsible for much of that detail. A lot of the procedures have been passed down from one generation to the next, or passed on from school to school. But many of these procedures seem designed to put hoops and hurdles in the way of the ordinary classroom teacher.

Early teaching career – all hoops and hurdles

Often a new Head will bring ideas from his old school and present them to eagerly nodding governors as initiatives. More changes for the classroom teachers to absorb. Come forward, Godfrey.

We mentioned on Tuesday how, even before he starts teaching lessons on his subject, Mr Godfrey has to take a 20-minute Form Group once or twice a day to register them as in for the day and to hand out messages. It all takes extra time at the start of his busy day and just at the time he doesn't need it.

Even the way classrooms are set out can assist the Mission. At primary school, you'll be used to one main classroom, one main teacher, you sit at the same desk, keep your books and pens under its lid – so there's not much excuse to forget things. Mission-wise, that's restrictive. And if there's ink on your books and gum under the desk, your teacher will know exactly who to blame. But at secondary school these days, as we said, you'll be in different rooms, at different desks – there's just much more room for manoeuvre.

In the olden days, secondary pupils had their own desks in a set room and the teachers came to them. Each pupil had his own text books, neatly wrapped in brown paper with his name clearly marked on the front and were always kept in his own desk. No time wasted handing books out at the start of lessons, no time wasted going to other classrooms to look for books. *Book* tactics were very rare. There was no opportunity to scribble on pages, tear the backs off them or any other underhand stuff. You couldn't – YOUR name was all over YOUR book. Although families had less money in those days, boys rarely lacked pens, rulers and all the necessary equipment for a smooth lesson because they had their own desks in which to keep them. And you couldn't switch desks to confuse a NEWT as you'd be separated from your own stuff.

There was no pushing and shoving outside classrooms pre-lesson as you were already in the room; no bell rush as only the teacher needed to leave. OK, there would be a period of time on your own as one teacher left and another came in, but any excessive noise could be pinpointed to your room, your class. You were told to sit quietly between lessons. Any commotion would soon come to the attention of a *corridor creeper* – a nosey prefect alert to anything that moved. There was no hiding place. So most boys spent the three or four minute gap between lessons to check homeworks, or to glue the soles back on their PE shoes.

As for the teacher, although he didn't have his own room, this didn't seem to matter as he had a quiet Staffroom with no boys to interrupt him, a place to relax or plan his lessons. Nowadays, some schools are even talking of closing Staffrooms.

What about setting, Sir? Don't we need to be in different rooms when we are split into different sets? Like if I'm good at Spanish and he's not.

Nice point, gentlemen. Today, schools sometimes split everyone up according to ability, lesson by lesson. But when you think about it, the whole principle of comprehensive education is that the strong and weak pupils share their experiences. In the olden days *different-ability* groups were arranged at the start of each year and within these groups there was less discrete setting. If you were generally a top set pupil, but no good at French, you had to go with Le Flow. Mission-wise there was an element of self-policing, the engagement of the more dedicated learners rubbing off onto pupils who might otherwise be distracted during French.

All these hurdles, all these changes… are they really for the better? You bet! The betterment of the Mission, that's what! Not like the good old days, eh Godfrey? Today, teachers like Godfrey have their own classrooms and once the Mission takes hold, your own classroom is your prison, isn't it Godfrey?

But Godfrey's stress and self-doubt started a long time before he'd ever stepped inside a classroom of his own.

When the self-doubt starts.

Where and when, gentlemen, do you think teacher self-doubt first sets in? After our Mission Musketeers have been at them? Certainly. But, doubt starts even before this. Again the system works in the Mission's favour.

Insecurity is a key part of teacher training. Before they go anywhere near a school, most people wanting to be teachers will have had to have spent years doing degrees or diplomas in their specialist subjects. They may even have carried out research to help to develop everyone's understanding of their subject; they are keen, well-rounded; they are successful. They're knowledgeable and confident. Successes every one, with lots of bits of paper to prove it. Ready to face the world. Then they look to a career in teaching, so the system has to knock that out of them.

To start they take what is called a postgraduate teaching degree or diploma. Now, gentlemen, most post-graduate courses for other careers acknowledge the specialist skills the students have already gained over three or four years at University. Well qualified – these graduates are treated professionally. Mr Godfrey's undergraduate friends were equally confident when they started their postgraduate courses, going on to enjoy interesting careers in economics and science, politics and law, where generally they were in control of their projects and their workloads. But Mr Godfrey chose teaching.

Prospective teachers are warned not to be so self-confident

– from the start. From day one the physical and psychological pressure on the poor student teacher starts to grow.

Ready, Godfrey?

Yes, Vice-Principal. I think…

You mustn't think, Godfrey. Well not too hard. You're gasping a bit at the thought of what's coming, Godfrey. Take a deep breath, lad. Remember how your first interview for the teacher training course went, everyone being positive and welcoming – and how it changed once they had arranged your enrolment fee. You arrived, that first day on your PGCE course? Remember? Around 200 prospective student teachers gathered in that main lecture hall at the University. Expectant. Keen. Ready to start their new careers. What was it, Godfrey, that the Director of Education said to the assembled students that very first day?

There… SPLUTTER… will be… ee … SPLUTTER… tea…

Go on Godfrey, cough it out.

They said, "There will be tears."

And did the course bring tears to your eyes, Godfrey? Are you nodding? No, you're shaking your head? In despair, perhaps. And what else, Godfrey?

VP, they seemed sorry that some of us didn't have seats. "This hall is packed today and some of you are standing in the aisles. Don't worry; everyone will have a seat come next June. Those of you that are left!"

A HUSH ALL AROUND THE ROOM.
QUIET SOBBING FROM MR GODFREY.

Gentlemen! Gentlemen, I know. In what other walk of life do they question your choice of career on your first day? Would a director from any other sector of industry or commerce, faced by a room of bright, enthusiastic, educated graduates, start with such a downer? If Mr Godfrey had wanted to be an analytical chemist, or a zoologist, a historian, a librarian; would they have said on his first day "there will be tears"? Hardly.

However, the education director was right, wasn't he Godfrey? A practical, realistic man, that director, wasn't he? Then he gave all of you a postcard. This one in my hand.

It tells student teachers that when things are getting them down there's a helpline to call. Who wants to start a job where it's generally well understood that it's probably going to make you depressed?

But Godfrey, you went away thinking "the director can't mean me". In fact, his words inspired you to gird your loins and face what was to come. True, there'd be weeks and weeks of lectures and long evenings of assignment writing. You were used to hard work. You'd get through it. You'd go for 'A's in your assignments.

You looked forward to teaching practice, where you would take your first steps in an actual classroom. Two placements at different schools lay ahead. Exciting, what? Oh, if ever a practice didn't make perfect, then it would be teaching practice.

True, Godfrey your first school placement seemed OK. People were helpful, you had a couple of weeks where you just observed more experienced colleagues; and when you started teaching you spent only about a third of your time with pupils. It eased you in so to speak; the training is cunning! For every lesson you had to give, you had two hours to prepare it. The school kept things easy for you, giving you classes with top sets, year 7s and sixth formers; lots of boffins all willing to learn. Also you had a kind and generous mentor who guided you through any hiccups. That was your first term!

Then they upped the ante, Godfrey, the teacher training university gave you a second placement during which you had twice as many lessons. For every two hours you had to teach, you had only one hour to plan it all. It got worse.

Gentlemen, just look at Godfrey, suddenly he had lots of books to mark. His evenings were no longer his own; his weekend off started on a Sunday afternoon around 3pm. But he had come so far. Godfrey began to cross off the days remaining until the end of his course. May as well struggle on and get the teaching qualification.

On top of all of this, Godfrey had been given those standards to meet (dozens of them), one of the main ones being to always have high expectations for learners. His second mentor was a model here; the mentor's expectations of Mr Godfrey were so high, poor Godfrey was given a mountain to climb.

OK, criticising Godfrey's mentor is a bit harsh. After all, the young mentor had his own career to think about, his own self-doubts to drive out, his own Head to impress with his fine pedagogical knowledge. And if he could demonstrate a bigger gap between a well-qualified and obviously intelligent Mr Godfrey and himself, then it might boost his own image in the eyes of his school. All boded well for Mr Mentor.

At the end of term, Godfrey had scrambled through it, helped by his fellow PGCE students, many of whom had had similar unsympathetic mentors, and he struggled across the line. The course director had been right. Only about half of those students on that first day in Godfrey's group eventually passed the teaching practice. The more fortunate failures had wasted up to a year; those less fortunate had wasted away. Stress-wise, those that had got through had it worst of all – they now had to look for their first teaching job. Yes, question over there?

Sir, please give Mr Godfrey another tissue.

Job hunting – it's a jungle out there.

By now Godfrey had invested so much physical and emotional energy in his teaching career that he just kept on going. Armed with his PGCE scroll, he could look for a job. He didn't have to look far. Every week, as we said, the teachers' own paper, called The TES, advertises vacancies at hundreds of the most wonderful schools in the country, where the pay is above average and the children are angelic.

Hunting for your first secondary teaching job, gentlemen, well it's a jungle out there. A right wilderness – and the prospective new teacher is unarmed, unprepared, all alone with the big beasts circling.

Outside of education, the first part of the process in getting a job is usually to send the employer a letter to say why you want to work for that firm, attaching a page outlining your qualifications and experience; this page they call a CV. You can use the same CV with small changes for different prospective employers. Then if they think you might fit the bill, the company will ask you to visit them to chat about the job at an interview. Most companies interview different people separately, usually on different days so as not to cause any uneasiness. A few days later the applicant might be offered a position; and this usually gives them a few days to look at other jobs before accepting or rejecting the offer.

Not so in teaching. Schools are NO-CV zones. Every school seems to have a different application form and you need to put aside a weekend to fill it in. Then, a personal statement to say why you are suited to your chosen school. Applying to two or three schools? Lock yourself away for the weekend.

But if you're lucky to get an interview… start taking the tranquillisers. Teaching interviews are like no others; the candidates are made to wait in the Staffroom, TOGETHER, stewing. Half a dozen prospective teachers, all nervously making small talk, appearing supportive of each other, yet actually weighing up their own chances against that awesome lady over there who is certain to get the job (usually in her thirties, well experienced, returning after having had children). Then each applicant will be asked to give a lesson to a group of children, hand-picked for their patience, while being closely observed by an SLT, hand-picked for their lack of patience.

After the interview, the prospective teachers, their nerves shattered by the intense pressure of the day, travel home… and wait. And wait. For *The Call*. For most *The Call* is abrupt and final. For one it's an offer; an offer the teacher has no time to think about. Take it or leave it. Can you ask for more money? At this stage forget it. Dilemma; do you take the St Trinian's offer or try for that nice school up the road.

AUDIBLE YAWN.

I'm coming to the point, young Sirs. To cut a long story short, eventually Mr Godfrey got his first job, didn't you Godfrey. It wasn't the school he wanted, it wasn't the town he wanted. But it was a job. And, to be honest, by now he was keen to start, weren't you, Godfrey?

Oh dear Godfrey, you got all your teaching files together, a new suit and a six-pack of ring binders – one for each class you'd teach – and you made an appointment to go in over the Summer holidays to see your new classroom and to learn a little about the delightful pupils anxiously awaiting your words of wisdom. You met one or two of your new colleagues in the Staffroom, were introduced to the hot water dispenser, given a badge on a string, and shown where the hoover was kept.

Then the new term started. A new set of hurdles suddenly rose up in front of you. Qualified Teacher Status standards. Godfrey thought that he was already a teacher having got through teacher training. But like the rest of the NEWTs he found that he wouldn't really, really be a teacher until he had spent at least a year at his first school meeting another 40 standards. At this school, his mentor was a slightly more mature person, sensitive to working with new teachers, who saw Godfrey as a future part of the team. At this school they were all in it together. Godfrey had arrived.

Remember Tuesday, Godfrey's typical teaching day from 6am to 9.30pm. During this first year, called QTS (his Qualified Teacher Status year), Godfrey also attended INSET days, weekend courses, extra after-school meetings with his mentor, extra, extra after-school meetings with his Department Head, and was rigorously observed by his Assistant Heads to make sure he was having high expectations of his pupils.

Nearly finished, gentlemen. At times it will seem to new teachers that every part of the system, everybody in authority is on their backs prompting and pushing while their hands are firmly tied by procedures. As we said, putting hoops and hurdles in their way at every stage, piling on the extra jobs, piling on the pressure. And criticising them at each and every turn. Constructively, of course.

I could go on, and on and on. OK, gentlemen. You may wonder why I'm telling you all of this. We are NOT here to be sympathetic to old Godfrey. Far from it. It's to help you to realise that by the time Godfrey sees you in the classroom, he has been through so much criticism, stress and self-doubt from the training, observations and placement practice that he has forgotten that he spent years being a respected expert in his subject. The teacher training system has already halfway worn him down for you. But he's invested so much time in those two teacher training/ NQT years, notwithstanding the three or four years he'd already spent on his university degree that he owes it to himself to carry on. So here he stands before you, believing he's going to help you to learn. Bowed, but not yet broken. Well intentioned, but thoroughly stressed. Doubting his own abilities. Now it's up to you to apply the 3Ss to complete the job. When you've lined up your tactics and, as the ADVP might say, are good to go, he'll only be good for going.

Can we go, Sir?

OK, soon be break. Just wanted to point out the stress on teachers from training and high expectations. But it hardly ends there.

I also mentioned powerful people on your side working from the outside. Ones you might not expect to be involved in the Mission. They include the Press, Local Education Authorities, oh, and I almost forgot – the dreadfully nice folks from Ofsted.

Yes, lots of adults unknowingly are on your side all working to create self-doubt and stress in the ordinary classroom teacher. Many of them suspect that your teachers are not teaching you as well as they might; pupils today leave school and don't seem to have the basic skills, the right attitudes and the commitment required for today's jobs. Teachers just can't be bothered to put the fine education theories into practice. They must be in it only for the "short days", long holidays and the pensions. Such a poor attitude from pupils must surely be the fault of the teachers; you're not taught proper, like.

Properlee, Sir. Adverbs.

Now. Time for a break. As it's the final day, we have a real treat for you. A blast from the past. Something from the sixties and seventies – sticky buns and milk. And the pies on the side are out early. Tuck in. Then, back for Lesson 3, when we'll talk about other allies in more detail – including **our biggest outside Mission ally of all.**

RUSHING AND CHATTERING.

LOW VOICE IN BACKGROUND.
Nearly 'Big T time', Godfrey. Trust me, it's all in hand.

Super Mission Allies.

Welcome back, gentlemen. As we said last lesson, in essence, there's a real… Not now! Sit down. Well, you should have washed them! Why do you think they're called sticky?

There's a real belief out there that a lot of teachers are failing pupils. How can your parents and the general public believe this? Surely, most teachers want to encourage pupils to understand their wonderful subject. Teachers are intelligent, educated and, as mentioned earlier, have persisted through years of stressful training. They needed to be creative, dynamic and… innovative and thoroughly Outstanding to get the job, and yet people still think they are bad at teaching. Why? Who puts these ideas around? Look up at the board, now. Just look at these newspaper headlines.

SCHOOL CHIEF: 5,000 HEADS ARE NO GOOD. *(Sunday Times)*

TEACHERS ARE ENEMIES OF PROMISE *(Independent on Sunday)*

COMPREHENSIVES SYSTEMATICALLY FAILING BRIGHTEST CHILDREN. *(Daily Telegraph)*

SCHOOLS COMFORTABLE WITH FAILURE *(Evening Standard)*

'CRAP TEACHERS' *(BBC Breakfast programme)*

SECONDARY SCHOOLS FAILING PUPILS *(The Times)*

SMALL BUSINESSES VOICE CONCERNS *(OVER TEACHING) (TES)*

OFSTED CHIEF TELLS (TEACHERS) TO 'GO THE EXTRA MILE' *(Daily Mail)*

There used to be dozens of such headlines, appearing week in, week out. But while the media report the *crap* labels, it doesn't start there. So, who puts these ideas around? Men in grey suits, that's who. These are the folks that have Heads and SLTs tearing their hair out; teachers having sleepless nights; the school cat wondering where its next meal will come from. They are collectively the people that put most pressure on schools and that pressure inevitably sinks down onto the poor classroom teachers; can't fail to stress them out and make them doubt their own abilities. Great for the Mission. So who's feeding the media with such ideas? Who are they, these Super Mission Assisters? The Government, that's who. And they're the Government. They must be right. It's about time you learnt a bit about politics, gentlemen.

No, Sir. Not politics. That's worse than Maths.

Please, please… never link politicians and Maths, especially chancellors.

You'll have seen lots of politicians on TV – they're the main government who hang out in Westminster. They are helped by local authority politicians who know your town, your school. But why would they want to put the pressure on teachers? Well it's a natural thing for governments to do. Let me explain.

At every General Election, the opposition party politicians tell the people what's not right with the way things are run and promise "to change things if you elect us instead". So, gentlemen, when they first get elected to change things, governments have to look around and decide *what* they should change. Often the things they first change aren't the things the people electing them thought they might first change. Pretty soon the priorities of the people, like law and order and lower taxes, are reserved *for a Second Term*. This is clever of governments. It means that the people who voted them in to change whatever it was they wanted them to change, will have to vote them in a second time before they'll start to change it.

So what DO they usually change first? History tells us that in looking for things to change, governments – no matter which party is in power - usually settle FIRST on three things. Just three things… always three things…

- **Education.**
- **Education.**
- **Education.**

Education is easy for governments to change, doesn't affect foreign relations, doesn't offend the Europeans, nor the Eurosceptics.
Usually the first thing they change is their name. The Department OF Education becomes the Department FOR Education. Subtle, eh? What about the Department for Families, Schools and Education or the Department for Families, Education and Schools. The permutations are endless. Companies that print the government's stationery are never stationary.

Nearer home there are those local politicians to look after the running of schools in your area. It used to be mainly the Local Education Authorities (LEAs), but now Regional Schools Commissioners seem to be taking over. They also like to justify themselves by changing things.

Anything and everything is up for change. Even the way they describe your school. It used to be simple when your parents could choose between public schools and local authority comprehensives. But the choice got wider: Independent schools, the new Free schools (neither are free, nor totally independent), grant-maintained, local-authority maintained, Grammars, City Technology, Sports and Science colleges, Federations and nowadays it's the turn of Academies. No need to learn these titles as they change with every new government.

However well-meaning these politicians are, it's got to be a big learning curve. The system recognises this. So politicians, whether new to the job or not, have teams of civil servants to help them along with outside Advisors, Researchers, Statisticians and Think Tanks. Add to these hundreds of charitable groups and Trusts, all wanting to have their say on how best to educate you, what type of school to educate you in, what to learn, how you should learn it

There's just one further hurdle before politicians and their advisers get down to making the changes. How could the education system be underperforming if it was planned and run previously by the same national and local civil servants and experts that have now been asked to criticise it? The only conclusion must be that it's not wholly a problem with the system; it must be the people running the system. Teachers.

Which teachers? Which schools. What's the best way to show individual schools and teachers are underperforming? This stumped the politicians and educationalists for a few decades, until someone – possibly a football fan – came up with the idea of the comparison tables. They'd put the GCSE results of every school into School League Tables to see how well individual schools were doing, comparing the percentage of pupils that pass their GCSEs with A*s to Cs.

Lower than about 30% A* to Cs and soon outside political forces put your school into what they call special measures. The

Head and the teachers know the pupils, know the catchment area, know the aspirations of the parents. The politicians, several steps removed, rarely do. Even if they did, they couldn't swop a dozen bright kids from St Michael's for a few disaffected ones. So their only solution is to give the school a short time to improve and either merge them or close them down. Merging two schools into one is very popular with local authorities as their colleagues in finance and planning just love to get their hands on any redundant school playing fields.

A host of organisations and individuals now get involved: Ofsted, Her Majesty's Inspectorate for Education, education improvement experts, each in turn setting off a whole cycle of events that seem to give teachers even more things to worry about, more work to prepare for their inspections, more observations. Just extra stress.

So gentlemen, the government is perhaps our greatest ally in the Mission. I've put this on the board just to press home the point.

It is a truth universally acknowledged that a GOVErnment in possession of an Education Department must be in want of a change.

Nearly finished now, gentlemen, with all the political theory you'll need... need to know... yes? What is it?

Sir, you've made a mistake on the board.   Spelled the word government with both big and small letters.

Is this better?

You've still left the first two letters of governments big, Sir.

Just a little play on words, gentlemen, just a little play on words. Amuses Godfrey and the other teachers.

GO… GOVE. That doesn't seem funny, Sir.

You've never said a truer word, boy. Mission-wise he was one of the finest.

SHORT PAUSE.

So politicians and their advisors are our main allies in the Mission. They are always criticising teachers, always changing things – just adding to teacher stress. So let's wind this up before break. This morning we've considered all the outside help the Mission can call upon. It's nearly time for you to take up the baton, to carry on the Mission.

Lunch now. Lovely choice. As a reward for this week's efforts, some of your favourites are on the menu. We've sweet and sour chicken with fried rice or a more traditional southern fried chicken with French fries.

Sounds like a lot of chicken, Sir.

We have a lot of hens.

Oh, Sir?

Yes. As I promised some of your favourites are on the menu.

Our favourite hens, Sir? Not Henrietta Cluck?

Can't promise. Depends who we catch first. The main course will be followed by sticky toffee chocolate cake and custard with a scoop of double cream. Perk you all up. Then after lunch a bit of Mission formative assessment and the grand finale.

Huh?

Go on, get out there.

As they leave the room, the Rogers and Hammerstein classic 'You'll never walk alone' plays softly in the background.

Encouraging Signs – The Mission is Working.

Great lunch, gentlemen. Won't be getting many like that at your secondary school. Not with all this Jamie Oliver stuff. Well, we've done it. Reached the last lesson. A lot of theory this morning, I know. But just wanted to assure you that there's lots of help out there.

So let's have a quick review, then some encouraging news about the Mission, then we'll make our way for the last time to the Mission Tactics Practice Suite for the grand finale. On Monday, we explained that the most important thing in life is to make school life easy, to have good mates, like-minded, fun-seeking friends, have a laugh, and learn what you think you need to learn. That's what secondary education's all about, gentlemen. It's a well-known fact that children are naturally curious and engage well with new things. Things you see on TV, in the playground, when out with your mates. But secondary school hardly ever covers the things you're curious about. It's just an outrageous imposition placed on your young shoulders by educationalists who convince everyone, including your misguided parents, that such unnecessary subjects are important.

Outrageous. What is it, gentlemen? Shout it out.

Outrageous! Sir

On that first day at Summer Skool, the Major General went through the Mission. The 3Ss. By now you should know these off by heart. Can anyone give the Major General the first?

BRIEF PAUSE. FOUR SHARP MARCHING STEPS.
CHEERING.

Steady, men. Deep breath. Ready yourselves. Huh, the first of the 3Ss, men. Anyone? Go. You in the red shirt. Good man. Advance! Bellow it out!

Slow down the start of lessons, Sir, Major General, Sir.

Spot on. The first S of the Mission is aimed at slowing down the lessons, which leads to shorter lessons and less wasted time on irrelevant topics. Pick your teachers well. Should come naturally. First dip your toes in with the NEWTs and TOADS. Don't spend too much time on the Awesomes and RETs.

As for the other two Ss, as we showed you last lesson, you won't be entirely on your own, you'll have a lot of help with these. Who can tell me what the other two Ss are? I bet you all can.

Stress and Self-doubt, Sir.

Good man, Curtley. All together, now, repeat after Curtley... what are they? Let's go... ALL TOGETHER!

STRESS AND SELF-DOUBT!!

Excellent. Bung-O! Slips off the tongue. Mission Musketeers, you've spent this week well. I'll have Mission Musketeer Medals for you all at the end.

Thank you, Major General, we'll let you get ready for the grand finale for the boys. See you in a bit.

See you later, men.

Don't know, as we've said Godfrey, they just like him. *[ASIDE]*

OK, settle now, gentlemen. And now for a final bit of encouragement. Something to demonstrate that the Mission is going to plan. To show you how the tactics from boys in earlier years are paying off. Wouldn't be much good telling you all of this theory about Mission tactics if we didn't look out for signs that it's working. It's what the Major General might call intelligence gathering. It's what teachers might call AFL, assessment for learning. Especially during their formative years. Little in-joke there, eh, Godfrey?

The Mission IS effective. The signs are all around. You just need to listen to Radio 4 (nah, you won't), OK then Children's Newsround on TV or just keep your eyes out for newspaper headlines like the ones coming up on the board now:

- **'GIVE US A LITTLE MORE RESPECT,' DEMAND STRESSED OUT TEACHERS.** *(The Observer)*
- **(GETTING) SECOND THOUGHTS OR JUST DAZED.** *(TES supplement for new teachers)*

- **GOVE COULD DO BETTER.** *(Teacher magazine)*
- **HIDDEN SCALE OF BAD BEHAVIOUR IN SCHOOLS** *(Daily Telegraph)*
- **CLIMATE OF FEAR EATS THE SOUL** *(TES)*
- **2000 TEACHERS SIGN PETITION** *(Independent i)*
- **IRATE TEACHERS THREATEN CIVIL DISOBEDIENCE** *(Daily Telegraph)*
- **NEARLY 50% OF TEACHERS HAVE CONSIDERED QUITTING** *(Independent)*
- **UK TEACHERS QUIT IN RECORD NUMBERS** *(Observer)*

There are so many of these headlines, week after week, in the papers and on websites. Changes here, changes there. Teachers revolting. The public believing they're revolting. Then, although you pupils won't see these, the Teachers' Unions seem really worried. It's not so long ago the NUT sent this to members:

> *"Michael Gove has confirmed his intention to mount a wholesale attack on teachers' pay and conditions – tearing up the national pay scales, removing pay progression entitlements, and ending pay portability (keeping your place on the spine when you move schools.) This comes on top of oppressive Ofsted and appraisal regimes, ridiculous bureaucratic workload demands, and a Chief Inspector of schools who believes that "teachers don't know what stress is". I believe that every teacher wants the NUT to stand up for members against these attacks."*

There you have it, in a NUTshell, the unions are well aware of what those in power are doing to help the Mission. Stress! Stress! Stress! We're winning, gentlemen.

The editor of TES described a "*TSUNAMI OF FURY*" about

to hit schools from disillusioned teachers. But, they can moan all they like. We have the big guns on our side. It was reported a while back that the head of Ofsted implied that he would help our Mission and put more stress on teachers to perform. He believes "Britain's schools have tolerated mediocrity for too long" and is quoted as saying "If anyone says to you that staff morale is at an all-time low, then you know you are doing something right." He's even got Ofsted to change the school grades. Schools that used to be graded satisfactory are now termed "requiring improvement". Same school, same performance but that new name implies they're no longer satisfactory. Again something to undermine the teachers' confidence.

And we've even had the ex-Education Secretary (boss of Department of Education) onboard, 'cos he thinks that among teachers there is a "culture of low expectations" and he promises that under his government teachers will be "in the firing line". "The quality of an education system can never exceed the quality of its teachers", he says and state school teachers need to catch up with the Independents.

Talking of big guns, they've also talked about bringing in a fast-track *Troops to Teachers* scheme to help with discipline. All these extra Awesomes around. Sure to knock back the self-belief of some ordinary teachers.

And the effect of this continuous criticism of otherwise professional, well-educated teachers who we've already shown are committed, and initially EN-THU-SI-ASTIC must eventually make them start to doubt their abilities. The government, national newspapers and lots of education experts are all inadvertently helping the Mission.

Look around your school for signs. They are there – right in the heart of where teachers try to get away from the stress. I know we said you'll rarely get inside the Staffroom. But if you ever do, just look at the slogans on the walls.

You'll see things like:

- IF THEY DON'T LIKE WHAT THEY'RE GIVEN TO DO, THEY'LL DO WHAT THEY LIKE!
- IF THEY CAN'T LEARN THE WAY WE TEACH, WE'LL HAVE TO TEACH THE WAY THEY LEARN!
- TEACHERS CAN'T ALWAYS REACH THEIR MAXIMUM, BUT YOU CAN ALWAYS RAISE YOUR MINIMUM.

All great signs. For the Mission. The Mission has well and truly penetrated a teacher's inner sanctuary. Finally, let's look at some statistics:

- 40% of teachers quit within 5 years
- 50% of teachers say "bad behaviour is a major concern".
- 40% of the NUT Union's teachers said their morale was low in a YouGov survey.
- And in another survey, half of the 230,000 NASUWT Union's teachers said they had considered quitting in the past year.

And, how's this for a headline? Sums it all up, really.

OFSTED CHIEF: TWO-FIFTHS OF TEACHERS QUITTING WITHIN 5 YEARS IS A 'SCANDAL'. *(Guardian, January 2014)*

All of this begs the important question what kind of training are they giving would-be teachers? Is the support they give new teachers really effective? And what about those that stick it? Why should well educated, intelligent, dedicated people have to put up with it? Why for 20 years hasn't someone in power done anything more to address the problem? The answer is that no-one has come up with an effective policy to frustrate the Mission. Gentlemen THE MISSION IS WORKING!!

Loud Cheering. Applause. Chanting.
The Mission is Working. The Mission is Working.

Plenary.

A Rip-Roaring Finale.

Well here we all are, back for the final Question and Answer plenary at Summer Skool, gentlemen. My how the week has shot by. We hope you've enjoyed it; we are sure that you'll do well. I've brought back all your lecturers – Mr Godfrey, the Major General, Mrs Shah, Mrs Benyana, Mr Higginbotham and the Assistant Deputy Vice Principal in case you have any last-minute questions on their specific areas of expertise.

Silence.
Coughing.

OK, then, gentlemen we'll get on with the… the grand finale. Yes?

Sir, if he's the Assistant Deputy Vice-Principal and you're the Vice Principal, then is there a Principal Principal?

Yes, but she's just called The Principal.

She? Where's she? Why haven't we seen her?

Just keep your questions to the Mission, not personalities. Next question.

Do they have Summer Skool in other towns?

Yes, gentlemen, it's a national scheme. We're everywhere. Our statistics show that around 93.75% of the eligible boys all over the country attend, or have been influenced to some extent by the Mission.

Don't think my cousin attended.

She's a girl, Dumbo!

Thank you, gentlemen, let's leave the interruptions for next term.

Sir, won't the Soldier Teachers be harder to use our tactics on?

I'll pass that one over to the Major-General.

Four Sharp Steps.

No worries. Suffrin' saxifrage, the troops are on your side. Spot on, men. Think RUTs, RITs and RETs; giving exciting lessons you'll want to go to. Practical and not so academic. And if you can enlist them in irrelevant conversations, they may even tell you tales of daring exploits on the battlefield.

No pressure on pupils; just extra pressure on their less-than-awesome colleagues.

Thank you, Major-General.

Sir, you said the school league tables were unfair to teachers. If the figures are right, how can they be unfair?

Good point. The figures could be correct, but all league tables are unfair. Just think to yourselves – which football team is the best? Of course it's the one you support. But they're not at the top of the league table. Yes, you – with your hand up?

School league tables aren't football, Sir. We've favourite teams, but we don't have favourite schools.

No, but your parents have. And they're not those at the bottom of the table.

So these tables are no good, then, Sir.

School league tables do tell you some things – like which schools are financially well-off, or have the best catchment areas, or the least number of kids with special needs. The highest schools in these league tables will be the Independents, supported by rich parents, the Grammars that select their intake from the top 30% of pupils showing early achievement, the schools with special politically-motivated funding, such as historically the grant maintained and now the Academies. It just seems a bit unfair.

What Local Education Authorities and their advisors don't always seem to take into account is the improvement children make while at the school. So if your school has lots of clever children then you are fairly certain to get a large percentage through with at least 5 GCSEs. But the less popular school down the road, the one into which the LEA have directed all the difficult kids, may get under 30% of pupils through GCSEs. It's hardly the fault of the teachers as it was the LEA that put all the low achievers there in the first place.

Anyway, the league tables show schools that look good and not-so-good, but it's hardly a level playing field. Some schools with low pass rates have talented teachers that work really hard with under-privileged, struggling children to gain a D while their grammar colleagues can coast along (I'm not saying they do) in the knowledge that their pupils will get A*s. When choosing which schools to criticise and close down, politicians and their local authority advisers don't always take into account these *value-added* aspects. No. That school's not got many GCSEs. The teachers mustn't care.

Next question. Yes, boy? With your hand raised.

What did you mean by value-added? Sir?

What's a level playing field?

I'll deal with that second question first. Sorry, forgot. Playing fields – a phrase rarely used these days around schools. Used to be something most schools had for boys and girls to run around on. Today, it's just a term meaning unjust. Any playing field that's really level nowadays is probably earmarked for a housing estate.

Huh?

Joke. Next question.

Didn't sound like a joke, Sir.

As I said before… ALTOGETHER… "never said …"

Never said a truer word, boy. *[IN CHORUS]*

CHUCKLING.

OK, your turn, now. What was the question?

What's value-added, Sir?

Good question. Value added figures show how much improvement there's been in your learning. Best illustrated by an actual case study. A sorry case. Mr Godfrey used to work in a socially-deprived area in a school that had over 40% children underprivileged and with special needs. There were very few boffins at this school. Well maybe one or two whose parents were very enlightened, or maybe they just didn't have cars. By any value-added standard, Godfrey's school gained reasonable results for its kids. Some of the best of what they call CVA scores in England. Pupils predicted Fs got Ds; those predicted Es got Cs. The two boffins got A*s. Unfortunately there were still not enough Cs to leap up the tables and… the local authorities put that school into special measures. Their improvement plans are meant to, well, to improve things but as we explained before, local authorities only think they are helping; many special measures schools aren't improved – they are closed down. Godfrey's school closed and he had to look for a new school. Sorry, I'm digressing again to tell you Godfrey's sad tale. Is Godfrey discouraged? No, just look at him – like most teachers he just tries to absorb the stress and get on with it.

Who's payin' for Summer Skool? All this stuff?

Just keep your questions to the Mission, eh? Next question.

BUT, SIR?

LOUD RINGTONE!

Saved by the bell, there, Vice Principal.

Touché Godfrey. One moment, gentlemen. Let me take this...

Thank you... everything's set up. OK. So are we, I think. Right, gentlemen. They're ready for us. It's what we've all been waiting for. The grand finale of Summer Skool.

FINALE.

OK, gentlemen, starting with the front row, we'd like you to pick up ALL your papers and walk purposely, two by two, to the MTPS rooms. When you get there, just line up outside ready to make a quick entry. Major General and ADVP – can you lead this group to their designated room?

OK, men, line up as if on parade. Orderly fashion.

Good to go, lads. You'll love this.

EXCITED CHATTER, FOOTSTEPS, SHUFFLING.
MARCHING FEET.

Hey, there's a chicken. Must 'ave got away.

MORE FOOTSTEPS.

Cluck, cluck… cluck, cluckkkkkkkkk!

OK, boys, stop that rushing around. No talking now. Be careful with those papers.

LOW RUMBLING.

Shoe lace over there. Told you not to drop anything. Keep up now.

HEAVY RUMBLE.
WHOOSHING NOISE, GETTING LOUDER.

Sirs, where's wi going?

MECHANICAL GRINDING AND CLANKING.

Are you sure about this, Sir?

OK, men, steady advance now. Shoulder to shoulder.

What the… ? I'm not going in there, Sir.

Can't turn back now, men. One final push to our final objective. That's all. Soon be over. Everything terminates here.

No, Sir, don't want.

Don't wimp out, boy. Last week's intake took it like men. Listen now to the VP.

OK, gentlemen. Line up there ready to enter. Can you bring him to the front?

SOBBING, MOANING.
SILENCE. ODD INTAKE OF BREATH.

Stand tough, men! You'll warm to this, trust me. Crack troops at the ready. Any volunteers? Need four to start; who's SAS material? Best feet forward.

HESITANT SHUFFLING.

Steady, men. Deep breath, you four. Ready yourselves. Go. GO! GO! GO!

Let's do it. Just go in!

DOOR OPENING. CLANKING GETS LOUDER.
OCCASIONAL WHOOSH AND A BLAST OR TWO.

THUD AS DOOR CLOSES.

OK, now the rest of you wait a moment 'til they're dealt with. STOP RIGHT THERE!!
YOU! Come back!!

Not goin' in, Sir. Leggit, lads.

Get him, Godfrey.

Come on, now. Let's just calm down and stand quietly over here.

Must follow orders, men. Or whole thing falls apart. Not as adventurous as our usual intake. A bit less daring than last week.

Door Opens. Noise Gets Louder. Door Closes.
Whooping and Cheering [From Inside the Room]

Vice Principal can you come and sort these men out, please? Allay any fears?

Thank you, gentlemen. Godfrey, go in and turn the machine off for a moment? Let's ask these four brave musketeers to help us. We're not going to force anyone to do anything they don't feel comfortable with. We'll let each of you decide. Just wait there until the first four get their breaths back. They'll tell you the delights they've experienced.

You four with the ruddy glow on your faces. Gentlemen, first impressions please.

Well good. Can I do his, Sir? Please, Sir, please.

Yes, but don't snatch at his bag. Oh, it's McNally again. Best leave him be. You can have another go with the leg-it boy's papers. The rest of you, gather round.

Great. Can we do it again? Pleassse, Sir?

Bemused Chatter.

One moment! Everyone listen up. I'll explain. As you know we don't want any of this stuff about the Mission getting out to parents and teachers. Just to make sure you don't take anything home unintentionally, Summer Skool has designed a pretty cool activity. Well actually it's a warm activity. Actually it's pretty hot.

Anyway, it's meant to be a fun surprise to end your Summer Skool with a bang. Just that today the bangs seem to be unsettling you. You boys, who've just been in. Can you elaborate, gentlemen, for this ultra-wary lot out here? Tell us what it's about. Then we'll all be more comfortable entering. You first, what did you find in there?

Well, it was really big.

Describe it properly, please. Think of your adverbs and adjectives.

Grey. Ginormously ginormous.
Big, red and green buttons.
Handles to pull on.
Heavy rollers, going round and round – really fast. Mushes your stuff up.
Things that pinch at you.

Nothing to be scared of then, gentlemen. OK, let's start to move in. ADVP take your lot forward.

Cracking. Right, my group, good to go, now! At the back of each room you will see a large, grey machine with green and red buttons. They're our Super-Shredders – specially designed to get rid of your notes. We call them *The Terminators*.

SHUFFLING FORWARD.

Once inside, I'd like you to line up on the side in fours and take any notes, worksheets, wordsearches – anything relating to Summer Skool – over towards the machine. Godfrey and the other teachers will help you if you can't reach the hoppers. But you'll all get a chance to press the buttons. Fun, eh?

Everything you need. Staple removers, paper grabbers, super-fast feeders, a boiling hot transfer-pipe from the shredder to the incinerator, paper mashers, hi-speed conveyor belts and... a nurse.

In line now, men. Up-two-three-four... up...

Super "Terminator" Shredder – every school should have one.

Grinding, Whooshing, Clanking.

Noisy Activity Goes on For a Good 20 Minutes, Punctuated by Odd Screeches, Whoops, Clangs and Laughter.

My tie's stuck Sir.

Get the scissors, Godfrey.

Further 10 Minutes. Machines Start to Wind Down.
Odd Clunk.
Grinding and Roaring Gradually Replaced by Increasing Chatter.

Then... Relative Quiet.

Thank you, gentlemen. That's just about it. Summer Skool is nearly over. Just one last instruction? We'd like you to make your way back to the main hall so that we can reward you all with a little memento of your time at Summer Skool.

Footsteps.
Five Minutes Pass by.

Let's just wait quietly for the others to get back. We want you all together. OK. Come on now, stop lagging. Ready everyone.

Well done, collect your mementoes as you come in, gentlemen.

Huh? They're football player tokens.

Look a little closer, gentlemen. They certainly are little silver tokens, made to look like World Cup player medallions. That's to confuse your teachers and parents should they get hold of them. Only we'll know where they came from. Now look carefully, round the rim of the coin. Teachers and parents never look there. What can you see? Can you see our slogans I AM A MISSION MUSKETEER and THERE ARE THREE Ss IN MISSSION.

GLEEFUL BABBLE.
SHUFFLING AROUND ROOM.
FEW COUGHS. THEN QUIET.

Well, gentlemen. That's it! It's been a pleasure teaching you this past week. All of your Summer Skool teachers have enjoyed your imaginative ideas and enthusiasm. Remember when it comes to our Mission, we are all here to help each other. Even if you forget things at first, they'll come back to you when you see the early adopters at your school daily practising our Mission tactics. By the second term of Year 7 most of what you've learnt here at Summer Skool will be truly embedded – tactics that will stand you in good stead throughout your secondary school life. One hundred and twenty boys from this one school, thousands from all the Summer Skools across the country, out there, waiting in anticipation for the new term, perhaps practising the Snitch and Snatch or the Bell Rush over the rest of the summer holidays.

Also out there this Summer, give a thought to the thousands of teachers, some NEWTs, some Oldies, one or two Awesomes. A new term ahead – on their kitchen tables, thousands of half-finished lessons, lesson schedules embellished with highlighter, well-thumbed behaviour policies. Your new teachers – all busy, all optimistically anticipating their new classes, all planning, all enthusiastic, all unsuspecting. Oh, what delights await!

Now, as on the other days, just be careful you aren't spotted leaving the gates. Don't ever discuss Summer Skool with your parents. It's our little secret. Don't ever let your teachers in on it. In their own time, they may realise there's something going on. Then again, maybe not.

Are we all ready to leave now? Good luck, gentlemen. See… you really are GENTLEMEN. All standing waiting to be dismissed. Let that be the last we see of such good behaviour. Go out and ply the Mission with gusto. Have fun – that's what secondary school is all about.

Boys and teachers join in with Alice Cooper's 'Schools out'.

SOME FOND GOODBYES. DEPARTING FOOTSTEPS, FADING INTO THE QUIET OF A CALM EVENING.

Skool's out for Summer.

Addendum.

The Secretary for Education, Michael Gove, left his post on July 15, 2014. Ofsted chief Sir Michael Wilshaw described him as "a transformative and radical minister of education." There are encouraging signs that his successor, the new Education Secretary, wishes to learn more about teacher workload. Heartening, yet early days.

Skool's really out for Summer.

"Quite disturbing news, VP! What, next week?
Surely Ofsted would give Summer Skool just a few more days.
At this rate, we'll all be good for going."

Skool's out Completely.

Teachers, please… just be careful out there.

APPENDICES.

A. SKOOL DINNERS
B. SKOOL WALL SLOGANS
C. SKOOL TACTICS
D. MEDIA HEADLINES.
E. SKOOL SONGBOOK
F. SKOOL PHOTOGRAPHS
G. SANCTIONS POLICIES WITH MORE THAN THREE
   LEVELS ARE FLAWED

Appendix A – Skool Dinners.

π Help yourselves to our delicious selection of savoury and sweet pies on the side

π A vegetarian option (V) will be available each day

MONDAY
- Turkey twislers with pasta
- Turkey twislers with rice
- Pasta and rice (V)
- Olympic ring donuts (lots of colouring).

TUESDAY
- Fish bricks in double batter, chunky chips and ketchup
- Potato cakes in batter, chunky chips and double ketchup (V)
- Chocolate bacon peanut butter pie (got that off the Internet)

WEDNESDAY
- Pork pie, buttered mash and mushy peas with a raspberry jus (got that off Master Chef)
- Rice, peas and pasta (V)
- Rumble crumble from the jungle. With large juicy grubs. (Ant and Dec again).

THURSDAY
- Fully-loaded, thick-crust meat-treat pizza and cheesy chips

- Margherita pizza and cheesy chips (V)
- Chocolate roly-poly with ice cream and custard

Friday
- Sweet and sour chicken, fried rice
- Southern fried chicken, French fries
- French fries in sweet and sour sauce (V)
- Sticky toffee chocolate cake and custard with a scoop of double cream

Appendix B – Wall Posters

STAFFROOM POSTERS.

- Catch them being good.
- Learning should lead to fun. And fun should lead to learning.

SUMMER SKOOL WALL POSTERS.

- Secondary Education is Secondary
- Academic: "excessively enslaved to principles, impractical" (Oxford Dictionary Definition)
- There's only one real ology – Tech-nol-ogy
- There are 3Ss in Mission – MiSSSion
- The Three Ss – Slow, Self-doubt, Stress-test
- Teachers occupy your space; you occupy their minds
- Teachers only look bigger (especially to Year 7s)
- Relax. You do the relaxing. Teachers NEVER can.
- MiSSSion-Musketeers – One For All.
- Combo tactics –All for One.
- Hey! Teachers! Leave them kids alone.
- It's what the Teacher Thinks YOU Think is Reasonable.
- When they can't work it out, there starts the self-doubt!
- When boys are all good to go, teachers are all good for going.

Appendix C – Skool Tactics.

CLASSICS
1. Idle conversation.
2. Relevant conversation.
3. No pen.
4. No exercise book.
5. Borrow teacher's textbook

PLAY BY THE RULES
6. Dress sense.
7. Registration.
8. Name games.
9. Cans & food.
10. Essential equipment.
11. School bags.
12. Arrive late with excuse.
13. Arrive early on your own.
14. Arrive early as a group.

GO COMBO
15. The 'Snitch and Snatch'.
16. Have a voice.
17. Happy clapping.
18. Phoney war.
19. Water, water – everywhere.
20. Loo breaks.

Be a Barrister.

21. Isms.

22. Equipment breakages.

23. Deflect the blame – onto a mate.

24. Deflect the blame – onto a teacher.

25. The 'Double Bubble'.

26. Self-deprecation.

Confusion Tactics

27. Playground Combos.

28. When we gotta get out of this place.

Confusion combos.

29. Be a borrower.

30. Go walk about.

31. Blinds panic.

32. Games.

33. Time's not right.

34. Bell Rush.

Special Times, Places.

35. Be computer literate.

36. Get interactive with the whiteboard.

37. Take close notice.

38. Corridors of power.

39. Assemblies.

40. Parental controls.

Appendix D – Media Headlines

THE MISSION IS WORKING.

- 'GIVE US A LITTLE MORE RESPECT,' DEMAND STRESSED OUT TEACHERS. (The Observer).
- SECOND THOUGHTS OR JUST DAZED. (TES supplement for new teachers)
- GOVE COULD DO BETTER. (Teacher magazine)
- HIDDEN SCALE OF BAD BEHAVIOUR IN SCHOOLS. (Daily Telegraph)
- CLIMATE OF FEAR EATS THE SOUL (OF TEACHERS). (TES)
- 2000 TEACHERS SIGN PETITION. (The i)
- IRATE TEACHERS THREATEN CIVIL DISOBEDIENCE. (Daily Telegraph)
- OFSTED CHIEF: TWO-FIFTHS OF TEACHERS QUITTING WITHIN 5 YEARS IS A 'SCANDAL'.
- (Guardian, January 2014)

Appendix E – Skool Songbook

- Tell me why I don't like Mondays (Boomtown Rats)
- Baggy Trousers (Madness)
- Revolting Children (From Matilda the Musical)
- Another Brick in the Wall (Pink Floyd)
- Let's get Ready to Rumble (Ant and Dec)
- You Can't Blame The Youth (Bob Marley)
- Never Miss a Beat (Kaiser Chiefs)
- Children of the Revolution (T-Rex)
- You'll Never Walk Alone (Gerry and the Pacemakers)
- School's Out (Alice Cooper)

SKOOL
PHOTOGRAPHS

THE VICE-PRINCIPAL

MAJOR-GENERAL
CUTHBERT-BUTTERWORTH

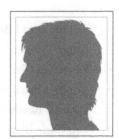

THE ADVP

MRS BENYANA

MR HIGGINBOTHAM

MR GODFREY

A MATE

THE PRINCIPAL

A BOFFIN

Appendix G –Sanctions Policies with more than Three Levels are Flawed.

Continuing the VP's Argument from Wednesday, Lesson 1

"The effectiveness of a school's behaviour policy, gentlemen, is inversely proportional to the number of sanctions levels. Standard school practices are biased against any sanctions level that does not involve the ordinary classroom teacher. Once the SLT become involved it can easily break down. You don't believe me? I know, there are all those lists of sanctions in your school diary. Just ignore them. Here's why you'll probably get away with it.

Let's say that a really naughty boy wanted to test the system. And that boy was you. First week of term, most teachers are unlikely to sanction as everyone is settling into the new term. But in the second week, you disrupt Mr Godfrey's class on a Monday. If he gives you a break-time detention for Tuesday, then don't go to it. You'll get away with it. Why? Because – especially if you can come up with a bit of an excuse - he'll give you the benefit of the doubt. A second chance. On the Wednesday (another break-time he's lost); you don't go to that either. So he applies a lunchtime detention. And you don't go to that. Again Mr Godfrey has waited in for you, missing a good part of his lunch and he's spent another 10 minutes writing a report to say you haven't turned up. Now he gives you an after-school, but after-school detentions involve more reports and letters including one to your parents to tell them you'll be held back (it was in the agreement they signed).

Some schools have a 48-hour notice rule as not all parents have email and the postman takes two days to deliver, so the earliest day for your detention will be in the following week, say the Tuesday. Mr Godfrey prefers after-schools on the Tuesday because Monday evening often involves an hour-long Staff Meeting, also it gives him time to remind you on the Monday that you have a detention on the Tuesday. You could at this time bring in a letter from your parents to say that the allotted evening is inconvenient. That might get you more time, but let's say you don't play that card just yet. Tuesday comes, but you're not there, again. Another report for Mr Godfrey to write, more of his time wasted.

So Mr Godfrey takes the matter to the Level 3 and reports you to the Head of Department, the HOD, who runs after-school detentions on a specific day of the week, let's say these are on a Wednesday. It's highly likely that the problem won't leave Mr Godfrey just yet as almost any evening the HOD could be called in to a management meeting, so she asks Mr Godfrey to sit in for her detention session. Only fair, after all it was Mr Godfrey who caused the problem by reporting you.

This is three weeks after you were first sanctioned. But again you don't turn up. The HOD will refer you to the SLT for their after-school detentions, which take place on a Wednesday or Thursday. Again because of the postal service and the 48-hour rule, your name will be down for an after-school detention not that week but the next week, four weeks after your initial sanction. By now sanctions have become a bit confusing for Mr Godfrey. Your personal sanction a month ago is clouded by all the other sanctions since, maybe involving dozens of boys and forming a complicated sanction pattern with some boys turning up on the wrong days, others not at all. Everyone at different sanction levels. Needs sophisticated software that kind of thing. By now Godfrey has forgotten why he sent you for detention in the first place and doesn't want to be bothered with you anymore.

You have effectively gained four weeks. And as this is a Level 4 detention with the SLT you will probably have to go to it. However, don't worry. You probably won't be asked to go to it. There's a good chance that the senior teacher is the Deputy Head. In many schools sanctions with Deputy Heads don't often happen. At least one evening per fortnight will involve the Deputy Head and SLT in after-school activities such as Parents' Evenings and Music Concerts. So the four weeks between offence and sanction typically might become five.

Now, school terms are on average seven weeks long and assuming you are not sanctioned in week one, then these five weeks take you to the last week of term, when often there are exams or special events for Christmas or Easter. And few after-school detention sessions are held at that time anyway – everyone's demob happy. The Deputy Head doesn't take detentions over to the next term. He prefers a clean slate.

In a nutshell, the boys that tough it out and don't attend detentions get away with it. After a term or two at a new school, classroom teachers such as Mr Godfrey realise that the detention system can't really work, so they become discouraged, doubt comes in "why doesn't the school behaviour system support me?" and they wise up and cut down on giving detentions. And, gentlemen, that's why any sanctions policy with more than three levels is likely to break down."

About the Author...

Writing under the pseudonym Edmund Irons, the author admits he spent his first year in teaching 'all over the place': on supply, on short-term contracts, daily assignments, in nearly a dozen schools, in three different counties. No matter where he worked, pupils seemed to use similar 'tactics' to interrupt his carefully prepared lessons. A subsequent full-time career in state secondary schools only served to confirm his early observations and conviction that to master the art of low-level lesson disruption, pupils must be attending special classes – but how, when and where?

Edmnd Irons spent twenty years as an industrial editor and copywriter producing numerous short books, feature articles and newsletters for science, technology and environmental companies. He later re-trained as a teacher of secondary school Mathmatics and has spent a decade teaching and tutoring.

Thank you for reading Summer Skool. Please leave a review, and if you agree that teachers are over-worked and under pressure, please continue to discuss it on Facebook, Twitter and in all relevant social media groups.

How changes come thick and fast in education? So much so that since Summer Skool *originally went to press, quite a few more changes have been planned for schools, teachers and not least – with the proposed move to 'All-Academies' – the LEAs.*
EDMUND IRONS, May 2016.